PRAISE FOR
SHORTCUT TO A MIRACLE

If you apply what this book teaches, you will find the Greatness within you.

> DEEPAK CHOPRA, M.D.
> Author of *Ageless Body, Timeless Mind,*
> *The Seven Spiritual Laws of Success,*
> *Way of the Wizard,* and *Peace is the Way*

It has been said that in order to be a realist we must believe in miracles. Miracles are a fact of life—events that are majestic and transformative, which appear as a grace and which connect us with the Divine. This book will help anyone understand the central place of the miraculous in the life of every human being.

> LARRY DOSSEY, M.D.
> Author of *Prayer is Good Medicine, Healing*
> *Words,* and *Healing Beyond the Body*

Are miracles possible? This fascinating book walks you step by step through the Laws of the Universe and shows through actual stories of miracles how you can use these laws in your own life. If you want to set your dreams in motion, *Shortcut to a Miracle* is a wonderful guide.

> SUSAN JEFFERS, PH.D.
> Author of *Feel the Fear and Do It Anyway,*
> *Embracing Uncertainty,* and *Life is Huge!*

Shortcut to a Miracle illustrates clearly that we have a power within us in our own lives. Not only does it show how changes in our attitudes and thinking can change our own lives, this book shows the reader a step-by-step process on how to do this.

GERALD G. JAMPOLSKY, M.D.
Author of *Love is Letting Go of Fear,* and
Simple Thoughts That Can Change Your Life

Shortcut to a Miracle is a book of hope. It renders the ordinary as miraculous and suggests that the lawful universe is ready to offer us sustenance. Providing instruction and support, *Shortcut* will help many relax into faith, trust and success.

FRED LUSKIN, PH.D.
Author of *Forgive for Good*
Director and Co-Founder of The Stanford
University Forgiveness Project

Shortcut to a Miracle is packed full of insights, techniques and tools for virtually everyone. Read it, apply it and life will become ever richer.

JOE BATTEN, M.S., C.P.A.E.
Speakers Hall of Fame
Author of *Tough-Minded Leadership* and
The Master Motivator

This book is a gem! Each chapter is a facet sparkling with wisdom. You can easily follow the specific guidance, based on proven principles, that leads you step-by-step into an evermore fulfilling life!

CARLETON WHITEHEAD, D.D.
Author of *Creative Meditation*

A STARTLING EXPERIENCE! This book gets right to the point. It offers you the unique chance to transform your life... then miracles truly happen and you will never again be the same!

JAMES KAVANAUGH
Author of *God Lives: From Religious Fear to Spiritual Freedom*

This book offers the religious as well as the non-religious reader simple yet effective techniques for achieving goals and the greatness within themselves. This book opens their life into a new beginning with ease, simplicity and grace.

GLENDA E. FLEMISTER, M.D., F.A.C.P., F.C.C.P.

The authors convey, with great simplicity and readability, a treasure of knowledge and spiritual understanding. *Shortcut to a Miracle* shows the reader how to move from being a victim to being a winner in life. It is an inspirational and life-changing book—one to read and re-read.

NIRANJAN S. SHAH
Member, Board of Trustees,
University of Illinois and
Chairman, Globetrotters Engineering Co.

Thank you, Michael and Elizabeth, for writing this awe-inspiring *Shortcut to a Miracle.* You've explained the unexplainable.

I've coached hundreds of workshop participants through the process of creating their own miracles, so the principles involved in the creation of miracles is not new to me. But I've never had the true path to a miracle explained so powerfully. This book needed to be written.

I've been showing others how to create their own miracles for years. I've known for most of my life that miracles are not a strange phenomenon, but merely the natural result of our having applied the three spiritual principles you've revealed to your readers in this awe inspiring book.

I doubt anyone can read this amazing book with an open mind and not be inspired with the awesome realization that he or she now has the ability to create miracles at will.

DAREL RUTHERFORD
Author of *So Why Aren't You Rich?*
and *Being the Solution*

SHORTCUT
to a MIRACLE™

THIS BOOK IS DEDICATED ...

With deep gratitude to all those
who have preceded us and brought
these Truths down through the ages;

With heartfelt appreciation to our mentors,
our teachers and our colleagues;

With loving support to all those
who follow and choose to walk the
path where miracles truly happen.

SHORTCUT
to a MIRACLE

HOW TO CHANGE YOUR CONSCIOUSNESS
AND TRANSFORM YOUR LIFE

Michael C. Rann &
Elizabeth Rann Arrott

Jeffers
press

A Jeffers Press Book

www.jefferspress.com

ISBN 0-9745776-8-5
Library of Congress Control Number: 2005927358

Publisher's Cataloging-in-Publication
(Provided by Quality Books, Inc.)

Rann, Michael C.
    Shortcut to a miracle / Michael C. Rann and Elizabeth
Rann Arrott. – 1st Jeffers Press ed
    p. cm.
    ISBN 0-9745776-8-5

    1. Success–Religious aspects. 2. Physics–Religious
aspects. 3. Consciousness.   I. Rann Arrott,
Elizabeth. II. Title.

BJ1611.2.R34 2005   158.1
                               QBI05-600037

Printed in the USA
First Jeffers Press edition published 2005

Cover and text design by Dotti Albertine

CONTENTS

FOREWORD

Dear Reader,

Are you ready for a challenging and joyful experience? Have you ever found yourself thinking, "This is going to take a miracle?" Are you ready for a mental and spiritual renaissance? If so, *Shortcut to a Miracle* was written for you.

This new book by Elizabeth and Michael is a real treat. Here you'll discover new insights into the immutable laws of the universe—*our* universe.

The authors believe, and clearly describe, why and how miracles are within the reach of us all. In my books over the years I have repeated *ad infinitum* that we become what we *think.* We become what we *say.* We become what we *expect.* This book provides an abundance of information about just how these things can be accomplished.

This book clearly guides you to understand what can happen—*miracles*—when you understand the natural and Spiritual laws of co-creation and when you decide to *become all that you can be* (a phrase I gave the U. S. Army years ago). At the core of it all is the recognition and understanding that what we call "limitations" do not really exist. A "limitation" is only an undeveloped strength!

Are you ready to create miracles in your life? You can! *Shortcut to a Miracle* will show you the way.

— Joe Batten, M.S., C.P.A.E., Speakers Hall of Fame
Author, *Tough-Minded Leadership,*
The Master Motivator, and many more

INTRODUCTION

If you've picked up this book to read or to browse, it's likely there is at least one area of your life in which you want some changes—possibly some big changes! Further, even though this area (or areas) is really important, it's also likely that nothing you've tried so far has brought about the changes you need or desire.

You may even have been telling yourself that "a real miracle" is the only thing that will bring about the changes you want because none of the "normal stuff" you've tried has worked.

Although most people don't realize it, we live in a world of miracles. We also live in a world of natural law and order. What most of us don't know, however, is that:

> The same laws that produce the natural order also produce what most people call *miracles*—those wondrous and unexpected events that occur when marvelous things happen in someone's life.

As you read this book, you will come to understand that we are already wired for miracles, and this means we are *not* victims in a ruthless universe—or at least, we don't have to be.

The principles underlying miracles have been esoterically known for many hundreds (perhaps thousands) of years, but the awareness of man's part in the miracle-making process is comparatively recent, having unfolded only in the past 150 years. Yet man's role still is neither widely known nor well-understood by most people.

This book is the result of the more than thirty years that each of us has spent studying the principles underlying miracles. During this same period of time, science has been unfolding the secrets of quantum physics.* This is the study of the strange world of sub-atomic particles— *the world within the atom itself.* As books on quantum physics began to be published that were user-friendly for laymen, we studied these books too, because we could immediately see that science was beginning to verify what our own practice and understanding of the principles underlying miracles had shown to be true.

A general understanding of quantum physics is still quite limited. Our children may be learning about it in school today, but when the rest of us were in school, it was scarcely understood by scientists, let alone by our teachers! Unless we were budding scientists, we studied classical physics as developed by Sir Isaac Newton three hundred years ago, which is accurate only to a certain point. Quantum physics goes far beyond that point.

We will discuss some of the many ways that quantum physics is very, very different from classical physics. Primarily, however, classical physics deals with the *visible* world—the world of form, the material world—and quantum physics deals with the world of the *invisible*—the world of sub-atomic particles, the world where miracles originate. Because some recent findings in quantum

---

*The names "quantum physics" and "quantum mechanics" are often used interchangeably.

physics tend to support the principles underlying miracles, we have incorporated some scientific history and findings in quantum physics into this book. This is particularly exciting because, until now, science and faith-based-anything have been 180 degrees apart.

While reading these findings, it is important to keep in mind that many of the conclusions that we, along with other well-qualified writers, present are not final. More research is definitely needed, and this can take many years. We didn't think you would want to wait that long to find out about this exciting work, and we didn't want to wait that long to write this book.

The book is divided into three parts. Part One provides the principles as to how miracles are created from a scientific(and) spiritual point of view. The combination of these two spheres—science and spirit—is breathtaking. Part Two shows how you fit into the miracle-making process. You will come to see that you are absolutely essential to this process. And Part Three provides the tools with which you can create miracles in your own life based on these scientific and spiritual principles.

You may find a lot of suggestions and ideas that are new to you. *Take your time in reading them so that you can absorb these ideas and then work with the suggestions.* You may even find some parts of this book that need to be read and re-read. We hope so. *These are the very parts that may be most instrumental in bringing about your miracle(s).*

Miracles *do* happen every day. In this book you will read about a number of people who have had miracles in their lives—wonderful things that have happened in the areas of health, success, relationships and prosperity. There's nothing special or miraculous about these people. They're people just like you who have found the way to their miracle, and, although we have changed their names to protect their privacy, they're all people that one or the other of us has personally worked with. We'll tell you about some of the things they did that opened the door to their miracle(s). You can do them, too.

If there is any difference at all between you and them, it might be that they believed in the possibility of miracles. Do you? If not, we think you will when you finish reading this book.

The possibility of miracles is true for all people, and it is true of everything in our lives—everything from the very big to the very small. The principles are universal, but the application of them is individual. You are the lead player; the stage is yours. This book gives step-by-step guidelines that will lead you to your own personal shortcut. These guidelines will help move you from wherever you are now to a life that is richer, fuller, more rewarding, and filled with wondrous events that we, too, call miracles.

Miracles are truly possible...for everyone!

— ELIZABETH AND MICHAEL
JANUARY 2005

NOTE: Although there are two authors of this book, we've written the rest of the book as though it had only one. We think it will be easier for you to read it that way, and we found through experience that it was much easier to write it that way.

xiv

PROLOGUE

In his wonderful little classic, *Acres of Diamonds,* Russell H. Conwell tells the story of a Persian farmer named Ali Hafed. Ali was a very contented man until one day when a Buddhist priest visited him. The Buddhist priest told Ali all about diamonds. He told him how diamonds were formed from deposits deep within the molten activity of the earth. He told him how valuable they were. Most exciting of all, he said that if Ali Hafed had even one very large diamond, he could purchase the entire county—and with a whole mine of diamonds, he and his family would be wealthy and powerful beyond measure.

Ali Hafed was no longer happy. He lay awake all that night thinking about diamonds. In the morning, he awoke early and went to see the priest once again. He told the priest he wanted to find diamonds, and so they discussed the most likely places where diamonds might be found.

Ali Hafed sold his land and with the money he received, he set out to find diamonds. He traveled and searched fruitlessly throughout the world. Before too long, all his money was gone. Finally, tired and discouraged, he came to the Pillars of Hercules where he threw himself into the incoming tide and was never seen again.

Meanwhile, a camel belonging to the new owner of Ali's farm accidentally unearthed a black rock with a bright eye of light. The new owner thought it was a very pretty rock and put it on his mantel. And one day, the same Buddhist priest visited him and saw the black rock with the flash of light. "Here is a diamond," he cried out.

"Has Ali Hafed returned?" When the new owner explained it was merely a stone from the yard, together they ran outside and dug into the white sand where they found other large, magnificent gems.

This is the true story of the discovery of the diamond mine of Golcanda, considered to be the most magnificent diamond mine in history.

Ali Hafed did not have to search the world for diamonds. Right where he was, there were many, many diamonds. They were already his.

This is a book about miracles. You do not have to search the world for miracles. Right where you are, there are many, many miracles. They are already yours.

PART ONE

WHY MIRACLES ARE POSSIBLE

I, 'I' in the widest meaning of the word (that is to say, every conscious mind that has ever said or felt 'I') am the person, if any, who controls the 'motion of the atoms,' according to the Laws of Nature.

— ERWIN SCHROEDINGER —
ONE OF THE FOUNDERS OF QUANTUM PHYSICS

CHAPTER 1

SPEAKING OF MIRACLES...

IN centuries to come, *the first half of the 21st century may well be remembered as the time when mankind first learned how to consciously make miracles.*

Throughout history, people have been told to "have faith" and "hope for a miracle." Today, however, the message is changing. Science and spirituality have begun to walk hand in hand, and this exciting new partnership has opened the door to a greater understanding of the wondrous events we think of as miracles, and how and why they unfold in our lives.

> **Any time your life, or my life, or the life of someone we know changes dramatically for the better through unexpected channels or circumstances, it's an example of a miracle.**

Philosophers and theologians have, for years, theorized about what it is that allows a miracle to unfold in the life of someone, and now the evolvement of quantum physics is beginning to demonstrate scientifically the validity of some of their ideas. As we begin on this path of greater understanding, some may still ask, "Are there really miracles?" Yes, of course, there are.

All of us have heard of miracles in the form of physical healings that cannot be explained by medical science. There are also miracles when the perfect solution presents itself at just the right time. There are miracles when some action taken by a person puts him or her in just the right place and results in greater good than ever seemed possible. There are miracles in finding the perfect job, the perfect mate, and/or money when it's most needed. There is no limit to the type and number of miracles that happen. Further, as you will come to understand by the time you finish this book:

> Miracles happen through natural and normal circumstances, and the "new science" of quantum physics is proving that we are—*every one of us*—already wired for miracles.

We can consciously take control and work to create a miracle or miracles in our lives. We are not victims of a random existence in a confusing and possibly hostile world. Life is for us, not against us. Not only is it possible to experience a dramatic healing or find the perfect solution to our problems, but it's also possible to express the dream or desire that we haven't dared pursue up to now and to learn how to bring such wonderful experiences into our lives more often.

HOW MIRACLES UNFOLD

Generally, a *miracle* is thought of as an event that runs counter to, or at least stretches, the laws of nature. It is often spoken of as an intrusion of the supernatural into the realm of the natural. Most dictionaries still use words such as "divine intervention" or "supernatural" in defining "miracle" or "miraculous." All of this is misleading.

In ancient Greece, playwrights developed a dramatic technique to help them solve impossible dilemmas in their plays. The technique, known as *"deus ex machina"* (God from a machine), usually involved a contrived solution whereby one of their powerful gods was brought to the stage via a mechanical device just in time to save the day.

In one form or another, mankind has carried forward the same idea from that day to this. In fact, this is probably behind the concept of Superman and other "super" heroes who miraculously "save the day" at the very last moment.

But *deus ex machina* simply is not the way miracles unfold. Think about it: No matter how improbable the possibility of a miracle may have seemed beforehand, after it has occurred, we are able to look back and see that it unfolded *with great ease and through natural means*. It may be astonishing. It may be synchronistic. But it is always a natural and amazingly simple unfoldment.

My favorite story describing this phenomenon is about a man repairing the roof of a tall cathedral. Suddenly, he slips and begins an out-of-control slide toward the edge of the roof. He throws his tools aside, and onlookers watch in horror as he continues sliding. They hear him cry out piteously, "God, save me. God, save me." There is a pause. He stops sliding. And then they hear him say, "Never mind, God. My belt got caught on a nail."

One of the oldest and most esoteric definitions of miracles was found on what is known as the Emerald Tablet, a single piece of emerald or green crystal believed by the early alchemists to date from the dawn of time and to contain the secret wisdom of the Hermetic teachings. The Hermetic teachings are thought to be the philosophical source of the great Mystery Schools of ancient Egypt that were subsequently studied by great philosophers such as Pythagoras, Plato and Plotinus.

The Emerald Tablet was translated by Alexandrian scholars in Egypt about 330 B.C. According to the second rubric (section) of the Emerald Tablet:

> "That which is Below corresponds to that which is Above, and that which is Above corresponds to that which is Below, to accomplish the miracles of the One Thing."[1]

What does this mean? Very profoundly, it is saying that everything in our visible world corresponds to a perfect pattern in the invisible world. Further, in some way, the invisible responds (or corresponds) to something in the visible world. All this accomplishes the miracles of a Unified "One."

The words of author Dennis William Hauck help to clarify this statement. In his book *The Emerald Tablet*, Hauck explains that according to philosophers and scholars of the ages, these words have long been understood to mean that the events of our lives, as well as those events that seem miraculous to us, are really the "natural interplay of the powers of the Above and the Below."

> "There are no real miracles, only manifestations of the universe's hidden laws that we do not understand."[2]

According to this definition, then, what is commonly called a "miracle" is really *a natural happening responding to universal laws.* And, of course, the more these laws are revealed, the better we understand them and are able to use them.

The reality is that we are using these "hidden laws" every day as we live our lives. However, to go about achieving miracles, what we want to do is to learn how they work so we can use them *properly.*

That understanding starts with looking back at the Emerald Tablet. "The Above," referred to in the Emerald Tablet, is, of course, the realm of Spirit where the creative action of Spirit originates; and "the Below" is the material world where this creative action manifests. This, then, is telling us that the "universe's hidden laws" are actually the Spiritual laws of creation.

Natural law is simply the manifestation in the natural world of the Spiritual Laws of creation.

This is what the Emerald Tablet was talking about. This is what "As Above, so Below" is all about.

This brings me to my own very simple, yet all-inclusive, definition of a miracle.

A miracle is a series of natural events occurring in the right sequence, and at the right time, to produce wonderful results.

So, then, we need to ask, "Is there really a *shortcut* to a miracle?" If so, what is it? Where is it?

Some people (a lot, in fact) may tell you that there are no shortcuts in life, but they are mistaken. There is a shortcut. Like so many things:

The shortcut is simple, but it's not easy.

It requires that we have the appropriate mental framework and the correct beliefs about ourselves and our relationship to life. This is what industrialist Henry Ford meant in his well-known quote, "If you think you can or if you think you can't, either way, you're right."

Further, even though something may look simple, the application of it may be extremely complex. To illustrate, one of the defining equations for Einstein's special theory of relativity is an incredibly simple formula, $E=mc^2$. Yet its applications have challenged the finest minds in science since 1905.

"Hey," you might ask, "is this going to take one hundred years too?" Of course not. In fact, you may well find positive changes in your life start happening very quickly as you begin to learn about the shortcut. But the fact is that while the shortcut is simple, its applications are complex and sometimes challenging.

> **The shortcut is understanding the "universe's hidden laws," and learning how to work with them.**

So, if the applications are complex, then why is it a shortcut? It's a shortcut because once we realize there are universal laws at work in producing miracles, we can let go of frantically trying one thing after another on a hit-or-miss basis, since:

**A law always works the same way
under the same circumstances.**

We can let go of being a victim because:

A law always works the same way for everybody.

We can let go of the fear that "it might not work," because:

A law always works.

So, what is it that makes the shortcut so complex and often challenging? The answer is as follows:

We work with these hidden laws through our thinking, and our thought patterns are complex. Incorrect or "limited" thinking can be difficult to recognize in ourselves and even more challenging to correct.

Still, although it may not always seem so, the fact is that we *can* have control over our thoughts. We can change even the most deeply-ingrained thought patterns and habits.

Actually, there are some similarities between the shortcut to a miracle (or miracles) and the shortcut of building a tunnel through a mountain:

- Both are simple but not easy.
- Both involve many factors.
- Both call for a lot of work, but the rewards are enormous.

There is, however, one very important difference:

Whereas, you don't reap any reward from a tunnel until it is finished, the mere process of starting to correct our thinking allows wonderful things to begin to take place in our lives. This opens the door to not just one miracle, but many.

THE HIDDEN LAWS AND MIRACLES

So, what exactly are the hidden laws of the universe as they relate to miracles?

There are many variations, but they all stem from one basic principle. Some call it the "Law of Belief." Others call it the "Law of Mind." I call it the "Law of Co-Creation." Essentially and briefly:

> The Law of Co-Creation is this:
> • Consciousness manifests.
> • Dominant thought prevails.

Consciousness is the sum total of *all* our thoughts, beliefs, feelings, emotions, desires and intentions. *Dominant thought* is our predominant belief or thought pattern about any given thing or area of our lives, amplified by the intensity with which we think about it. Therefore it follows that:

The more we are able to align our thinking with what we want, the more fully empowered we become, and the more transformed our lives become.

As we begin to live our lives and our dreams from a standpoint of conscious co-creation, we experience all of life with better health, more harmonious relationships and ever-increasing joy and self-fulfillment. We also experience miracles.

So, in some mysterious way that science is, as yet, only beginning to understand, we are actually the co-creators of our lives.

Here it all is, in a nutshell:

The Shortcut to Working with the Hidden Laws of the Universe As They Relate to Miracles in Your Life

1. We are, each of us, the thinker in our world.

2. We choose the thoughts we think, and we are the creator of our thought patterns.

3. Our dominant thought patterns manifest in our lives.

4. Therefore, we want to eliminate thought patterns that deny our good and create in their stead thought patterns that *establish* our good.

5. "Our good" is whatever we desire in life, so long as it does not interfere with anyone else's good. Each of us gets to define what that good is.

6. Once we come to accept that we are truly entitled to have good happening in our lives, and the good that we define for ourselves becomes a living reality in our minds, the door to the manifestation of our good is wide open.

7. The universe supports us fully in bringing the manifestation of our good to pass... guiding and directing us, attracting into our lives everything necessary for it to happen.

Although these guidelines are simple, their application is complex because each one of us is a unique and complex individual. And so this becomes a process for each of us, a serious commitment filled with rich and unexpected rewards—and miracles—every step of the way.

We will spend the rest of the book learning how these laws work and how to use them correctly.

THE MIRACLE OF OUR UNIVERSE AND OF LIFE ITSELF

Approximately 15 billion years ago, our physical universe came into being in an explosion of absolutely incomprehensible force. At the moment of this great cosmic explosion, searing hot energy that had been compressed into a speck smaller than an atom was released—enough energy to form all the matter that exists in the universe today. This, too, is virtually incomprehensible.

Planet Earth is part of the Milky Way Galaxy, a cluster of some two hundred billion stars. The span of our galaxy is 100 thousand light-years. (To figure out how many miles this is, multiply 100 thousand by 6 trillion.) We now know that there are thousands of galaxies within 100 million light-years from us, and billions of others within the range of our largest telescopes

And the universe is still expanding! Some of these galaxies are up to one billion light-years away and are moving away from us at speeds up to 100 million miles per hour.

Most astonishing of all—if, within one second of the "moment of beginning," the rate of expansion of cosmic energy had been different by plus or minus even one part per quadrillion (that's one followed by 15 zero's), you and I would not be here today. One part per quadrillion less, and the universe would have flown apart too fast for the galaxies, stars and planets to form. One part per quadrillion more and the universe would have collapsed in on itself before life could have evolved. In either case, we would not be here. Neither would anything else.[1]

CHAPTER 2

THE MIRACLE-MAKING ATTITUDE

BEFORE we can accept miracles in our lives, we first have to believe that there is a Power and an Intelligence capable of making miracles—real miracles—BIG miracles.

The same Power and Intelligence that made the first miracle—the miracle of the universe and of life itself—is the same Power and Intelligence that is responsible for all miracles. This Power is not random or capricious. It operates always in accordance with infallible Law.

There is no "large" or "small" to the Power and Intelligence that produces miracles. There is only one originating Source of all Power and Intelligence, and that One Source is Spirit.

Life, Power, Intelligence and Love all originate with the One Source. They all become manifest through Law.

And, as discussed in the previous chapter, natural law is simply the manifestation in the natural world of the Spiritual Laws of creation. So, take a moment and open your mind to the unfathomable Power and Intelligence that is responsible *for our entire universe, for all life and for all miracles.*

Try to imagine a speck smaller than an atom—one that explodes into an incredibly hot mass of energy, hot beyond anything we can imagine and of such unfathomable force as to release *in one instant* all the energy needed to form all the matter that will ever exist, even billions of years later. Within seconds, this energy begins to produce particles and anti-particles that after 300,000 years form clouds of hydrogen and helium atoms. Another billion years and these clouds form into clumps that become stars and planets, some very like Planet Earth.[1]

A cooling process continues for another two billion years, and over the next three billion years a process of biological evolution takes place on Planet Earth which ultimately leads to the existence of thinking human beings who are capable of knowing, understanding and appreciating all that has taken place.[2] *Can this be anything but miraculous?*

Just as a sailor learns to use the winds of the world to arrive at a chosen destination, once we understand the principles involved, we can learn how to use the Laws of this Intelligence and Power to bring great good into our lives—and miracles, too!

To do so, we must accept that this Power and Intelligence can, will, does and must respond to us.

BEGIN WITH AN OPEN MIND

Begin now to open to what may be a new way of thinking. Allow the understanding to unfold. An open mind is probably your most indispensable attribute. The recent scientific discoveries I'll be talking about later in this book point indisputably to the following truth, which has been esoterically known for centuries:

<u>Our mind</u> is the instrument of our miracles.

Because of this, the single most important aspect of having miracles manifest in your life is to know this:

Miracles can happen, and they can happen *for you.*

This simple statement—once it is truly accepted and becomes a belief or, better yet, a conviction—is the essence of having miracles in our lives. The degree to which we accept this statement is directly proportional to what I call our "Miracle-Making Attitude."

A MIRACLE-MAKING ATTITUDE

A Miracle-Making Attitude is comprised of five elements. Doubt in any one of these areas can have a negative impact on the manifestation of your miracle.

1. **Miracles unfold according to Universal Law.** Too often, people think that blind faith in an outside Power is necessary for miracles; and, further, that this Power is somewhat unpredictable—granting miracles sometimes and withholding at other times. Begin right now to know that miracles do not happen by chance. They are no more random or capricious than the infallible Law underpinning this entire universe. By the time you finish the first three chapters of this book, you will understand why this is so.

2. **Your miracle is possible.** Any time you question whether the miracle you desire is possible, re-read "The Miracle of our Universe and of Life Itself" on page 14. Think again about this awesome universe, and ask yourself if the incomprehensible Intelligence and Power responsible for creating this universe isn't far more than enough to also bring into your life whatever it is that you need or desire.

3. **Your miracle is never too big.** When you are faced with a challenge in your life, one of the things you may wonder is whether what you want or think you need is "too big." It is not too big! Ralph Waldo Emerson said it best, "There is no large or small to the Soul that maketh all."[3]

4. **You play a major role in bringing about your miracle.** You may wonder, "If it can happen, do I have any part in making it happen, or allowing it to happen?" Yes. It happens *through* you, not *to* you. Your part has to do with your belief, and your belief is the result of your thinking. And—this last point is especially important— you have control over your thinking.

5. **You deserve miracles in your life.** The final question you may have is, "Do I deserve to have something this good happen?" The answer is an unqualified, "Yes!" You deserve miracles because the Love, the Power and the Intelligence that created the universe also created you, and It created you to live and enjoy life as fully and completely as you choose. Regardless of anything that may have happened in the past, this same Love, Power and Intelligence is ready RIGHT NOW to respond to you in positive ways. To put this another way:

You are already wired for miracles.

Any question about whether or not you deserve miracles is strictly in *your* mind and does not exist in the Power and Intelligence operating behind miracles.

Whether it is the healing of an "incurable" disease, the solving of an "impossible" problem, the resolution of "irreconcilable" differences between family members or good friends or the turnaround of a "hopeless" financial situation, none of these is impossible. And the miracle-making process is essentially the same for each of them.

But since miracles rarely happen to people who don't believe in them, this Miracle-Making Attitude is vitally important to adopt. And the deeper your belief and the greater your conviction, the more fully your life opens to the miracles you desire. Miracles _unfold_—they're not coerced, and they're not forced.

Opening to this new way of thinking often means we need to let go of old thinking.

If we want miracles in our lives, we need to let go of old ways of thinking and begin seeing ourselves and our world in new ways so we can be open to accepting miracles.

This sounds deceptively simple, but letting go of old ways of thinking is _not_ an easy thing to do. In fact, it's very challenging because the old ways of thinking have "worked" for us, and if we didn't think they were right, we would have changed them long ago. Let's also be very clear that letting go of old ways of thinking has to do with _choice_ and _will_, not with intellect and brainpower.

There are two very interesting stories that illustrate what can happen with an open mind (and the ability or willingness to let go of old thinking) as well as what can happen with a closed mind (and the refusal to let go of old thinking). Both stories involve the same person: Albert Einstein, a man with one of the finest minds in all history.

This man and these particular stories relate to some of the early work that is only now unfolding to help us understand the scientific basis of what we call "miracles."

ALBERT EINSTEIN... WITH AN OPEN MIND

In 1905, Albert Einstein was twenty-six years old and working as an unknown clerk for the Swiss Patent Office. He had received his Ph.D. only two years earlier. In this one year, he made a spectacular entrance onto the world stage of theoretical physics by publishing five papers, three of which solved the outstanding problems of physics at the time. One even won a Nobel Prize.

One of these papers, entitled "On the Electrodynamics of Moving Bodies," was astounding for more than just the substance of the paper. *Einstein used no footnotes or citations and hardly any mathematics to come to his conclusions.* According to scientist and novelist C. P. Snow, "It was as if Einstein had reached the conclusions by pure thought, unaided, without listening to the opinions of others."[4] To a surprisingly large extent, that is precisely what he had done.

A later supplement to Einstein's paper contained what is probably the most famous equation in physics: $E=mc^2$ (energy is always equal to the mass of an object multiplied by the speed of light squared).

This ground-breaking work became known as "Einstein's special theory of relativity" and, to physicists, it explained many interesting and challenging concepts.

To us, looking to understand more about miracles, it offered two major tenets:

1. Energy and mass are somehow interchangeable.
2. Nothing travels faster than the speed of light.

Later in the century, particle accelerator experiments did, in fact, verify that mass and energy are *totally* interchangeable. This in turn led to the understanding that all matter is composed of energy and therefore is not "fixed" or "unchangeable." *This is important when thinking about miracles.*

All matter is composed of energy.
All matter is changeable.

The second tenet, "Nothing travels faster than the speed of light," later became instrumental in something known as the EPR Paradox. We'll talk briefly about the EPR Paradox later, but what is important to our understanding now is that it was the basis for this important scientific discovery:

' all is One'

Everything in the universe is interconnected.

This theory was called "Einstein's special theory of relativity" because it did not incorporate the effects of gravity. Einstein's big challenge, of course, then became to incorporate the effects of gravity—*and it took Einstein an additional eleven years to do this.*

The reason it took so long was largely because space and time had always been *assumed* to be a flat, fixed arena unaffected by the movement of other bodies and the action of natural forces.

It was only when Einstein finally put aside his (and everybody else's) belief in time and space as being fixed or absolute that he opened himself to unprecedented thinking. As he did, he made the revolutionary suggestion that the space-time continuum is not flat and fixed but is actually curved or "warped" by the distribution of mass and energy in it.[5] With this realization, he was then able to formulate what became known as his "*general* theory of relativity," which actually is important to our understanding of miracles.

This theory establishes that space and time are not static, but rather dynamic quantities that are *relative to the observer as well as to the thing being observed.* So they not only affect, but are affected by, everything that happens in the universe. In some fundamental way, then—

**Everything in the universe is
affected by everything else.**

Einstein's new theory accurately predicted the bending of light rays by the gravity of the sun, something that completely revolutionized the scientific world.

So, for three hundred years, science had lived by Sir Isaac Newton's view that the universe operated purely mechanistically, or "clock-like." That view had just been upset—all because Albert Einstein completely opened his mind and began to seriously explore previously unthought-of possibilities.

When Einstein let go of the long-held and universal belief that time and space were fixed, he was able to complete his new, groundbreaking theory. This theory opened the door for all of science to look at the universe in a more profound and accurate way.*

Like most of us, however, there were areas where Einstein was either unable or unwilling to open his thinking.

ALBERT EINSTEIN... WITH A CLOSED MIND

Today, most scientists acknowledge that our universe came into being with an explosion of incalculable power; but in the early years of the twentieth century, this was a subject of great disagreement between theologians, physicists and astronomers. There were two opposing theories about the origin of the universe.

The first of these was the "Big Bang." According to this theory, there was a moment of beginning, a point in time when the universe came into being through an explosion of incomprehensible force and power. But this led to the obvious question of, "*How* did this huge cosmic explosion come to be? Who or what made it happen?" The unmistakable implication, of course, was an Originator or

---

*The major search today, begun by Einstein decades ago, is for a complete unified theory (the "theory of everything") that will incorporate both the general theory of relativity and quantum mechanics. Science admits the challenge is great.

some Originating Force. While most philosophers and theologians supported this theory, most men of science, including Albert Einstein, were strongly opposed to it (as well as to the concept of an Originator or Creator). They felt very strongly about this.

The theory held by most scientists was known as "steady state" cosmology. That theory presumed a universe without a beginning and without an end, one in which dying stars were replaced by young, hot stars. It was a theory in which there was no Originating First Cause because there simply was no beginning, only perpetual balance.

Einstein's professional opposition to the idea of a universe that had "a beginning" or a "First Cause" is a fascinating example of how challenging it can be to let go of a cherished belief and open yourself to a new way of thinking.

This is what happened.[6] When Einstein finally finished the work on his equations of general relativity, he sent copies to some of his colleagues so they could apply the new theory to their particular scope of work.* Shortly thereafter, and much to Einstein's surprise, a Dutch scientist named Willem de Sitter responded, saying he had

---

*Scientific theory is always provisional, a hypothesis. It is developed mathematically and has to accurately describe a large class of observations. It also has to make definite predictions about the results of future observations. Other scientists, frequently in other scientific disciplines, work with these mathematical formulas to develop some of these predictions as they relate to their own area of scientific study. The predictions, in turn, are tested, either by observable evidence or laboratory experiment. If even a single observation disagrees with its predictions, the theory must be discarded or modified.

found a solution to the equations that actually predicted a universe in which the galaxies were moving rapidly away from one another. This supported the Big Bang theory, the very theory to which Einstein was completely opposed. Einstein initially dismissed this response as a weak understanding of physics on the part of the other scientist.

A short time later, Aleksander Friedmann, a Russian mathematician, found a mathematical error in Einstein's formula. When this error was corrected, the concept of an expanding universe was, once again, unmistakable.

> Einstein's own revolutionary formulas were supporting a basic concept to which he was unalterably opposed.

For over two years, letters and notes went back and forth, and both Einstein and de Sitter published contradictory findings in the *Zeitshrift fur Physik,* a leading professional journal. Einstein wrote openly of his annoyance with the whole issue.

Years passed, the issue remained unresolved, and Einstein remained annoyed by and dismissive of the continuing reports from his colleagues that his equations and formulas on general relativity were supporting the possibility of an expanding universe. An expanding universe could only support the theory of the Big Bang... and the theory of the Big Bang could only support the concept of a Creator, or an Originator. Finally, Belgium's most famous astronomer, a Jesuit priest named Abbe´ Georges Lemaître, discovered yet *another* area where these equations predicted a dynamic and expanding, rather than static, universe. This time, Einstein responded quickly by arbitrarily adding what he called a "cosmological constant" to his formula. Once more, Einstein had the universe back where he wanted it— in a static state, one where it was *not* expanding.

Lemaître, however, didn't like the idea of Einstein adding something "out of thin air," so he carefully prepared a scientific argument disproving Einstein's cosmological constant and managed to corner the great man during a visit to the Mt. Wilson Observatory. There he painstakingly presented to Einstein his mathematical theory of the "primeval atom."

Einstein sat quietly for a moment, then stood up and acknowledged Lemaître for having made a most beautiful presentation. He even went on to admit that creating the cosmological constant was the "biggest blunder" of his life. It was a touching admission by a great and brilliant man! But... *still* he held to his idea of a static universe.

Finally, on October 6, 1923, Mt. Wilson Observatory reported one of the most important discoveries in the history of science: Edwin Hubble had found unmistakable evidence that the universe was expanding in the aftermath *of a great explosion that took place billions of years ago.* His findings became known as Hubble's Law, "The more distant the galaxy, the faster it recedes from us." This meant that the concept of an expanding universe was no longer theory. It was now supported by *observation.*

Still, it was *another seven years* before Einstein finally acknowledged that it was "likely" that the general structure of the universe was not static. Even then, it was not until *another 25 years had passed* (in 1955, shortly before his death) that Einstein acknowledged to a visitor that he had finally come to accept the idea of "a beginning."[7]

Einstein's tenacity of thinking—his inability to let go of a deeply-held, cherished belief—in no way detracts from the staggering contributions he made to the world. In fact, it is his very genius—his extraordinary mental abilities and clarity of thought—which make this story so valuable, because it illustrates how challenging it can be to open to new ways of thinking which contradict long-held beliefs.

The point to all this, of course, is that:

There may be times when you need to let go of old thinking about how the world (and life) works. There even may be times when you need to let go of old ideas about yourself in order to open to new ways of thinking and new paths of healing, success or creative expression in your life.

Before concluding this chapter, let's take another look at the first three elements of a miracle-making attitude. (We'll be addressing the other two further in future chapters.)

- Miracles unfold according to Universal Law.
- Your miracle is possible.
- Your miracle is never too big.

Keeping in mind that the Power and Intelligence that created our awesome universe is *the same Power and Intelligence that is responsible for the miracles in our lives*, let's review some of the other important things we've learned in this chapter.

We live in an immense universe of Intelligence, Power and essential order and harmony.

If it were not so, the universe would have either imploded or exploded many millions of years ago, and we would not be here today. Additionally, for the first time in history, there is substantial scientific support for the concept of an Originating First Cause (the "Big Bang" theory). Further:

The laws of the universe do not change simply because we fail to understand them.

They are what they are. They operate the same way, all the time—and it is up to us to align ourselves with them. We are using these laws right now in the co-creation of our lives. Whatever is happening in our lives is a direct result of *how* we are using them. And...

If our belief contradicts the way things really are, we will *not* be on the right path until we change our belief.

That's the way it is with our thinking. Until we get it right, we are limited in our progress. For example, Einstein's groundbreaking general theory of relativity didn't change the world. It changed the way we *understood* the world. And until we got it right, we couldn't go any further.

Similarly, in order to make miracles, we need to align ourselves with the laws of the universe *as they exist.* It doesn't matter what we think they are, or what we would like them to be. We must open our minds to things as they are—and this may require embracing new ideas and concepts. Until we are able to do this, our lives will not change.

A deeply-held belief can blind us to things that are right in front of us. Furthermore, if the error of our thinking is pointed out to us but conflicts with a deeply-held belief, we often have great difficulty seeing it, acknowledging it and/or accepting it.

We can only wonder what quantum leaps might have taken place in understanding the deepest truths of the universe had Einstein been able to accept the possibility of the Big Bang theory years earlier.

Let us also wonder what quantum leaps might be possible in the lives of each one of us when we let go of beliefs that conflict with what *really is.*

Now, let's move on, to explore what happens when we stop trying to shape the world to our beliefs and, instead, align ourselves and our thinking with the laws of the Universe as they are rather than as we think they are.

CHAPTER 3

THE INVISIBLE LINK

IN this chapter, we move from the world of the *macro-cosm* (the visible, material world) to the world of the *microcosm* (the invisible, non-material world). It is in this incredible and fascinating sub-atomic world—the world of the quantum—that we find the invisible link to the Source of miracles. This is where we can begin to understand how and why miracles take place.

If you are like me and many others, learning even a bit about this strange, invisible world will help you to understand how the miracle-making process works and why it works the way it does (and why it can't work any other way!). If you want to make miracles in your life, you will probably have to make some changes, and, for most of us, it's a lot easier to make changes when we understand why it's to our benefit to make them.

First, some background. Almost 2,500 years ago, a Greek philosopher known as Democritus of Abdera theorized that at the smallest divisible level, all the matter in the universe might be comprised of very small invisible building blocks. He called this elementary building block an "a-tom," or "that which cannot be cut."

It turns out that Democritus was right. An atom *is* the smallest particle into which our basic elements (e.g., iron, copper, etc.) can be divided. Some two and a half millennia after Democritus, Richard Feynman, the brilliant Caltech physicist, said, very simply:

"All things are made of atoms."[1]

Atoms are very, very small. Feynman uses this example: If an apple were magnified to the size of the earth, then the atoms in the apple would be approximately the size of the original apple. And that's just the atom!

Atoms are composed of sub-atomic particles (also called "quantum particles") which, in various combinations, give the atom its individual characteristic. If the atom is small, these sub-atomic particles within the atom are incredibly smaller. For example, the nucleus of the atom, which houses the quantum particles, is only *one-millionth of a billionth* of the full volume of the atom.[2] The nucleus contains protons and neutrons, and also has electrons orbiting around it—and all of these are quantum particles. So, when we are talking quantum, we are talking *so small* that there isn't really a good word for it. What is so amazing is that:

We live in a quantum universe.

In *How to Know God,* bestselling author Dr. Deepak Chopra describes the realm of the quantum as the transitional place between Spirit (God, The Source, Higher

Power, First Cause) and the material world.[3] Thinking of it in this way helps us begin to comprehend the incomprehensible: How the Power and Wisdom that undergirds and permeates the universe moves into physical manifestation.

This mysterious, non-material realm forms an underlying fabric in, through and around everything in the natural world. Importantly, it is in this realm that our intentions, thoughts, desires and emotions begin the process of affecting not only our bodies but also the events and circumstances of our lives.

UNDERSTANDING THE UNSEEN WORLD

As we discuss this unseen world, we will look at three central points regarding the universe and our relationship to it.

1. Our universe is a universe of Law.

2. Natural law is the physical manifestation of a higher degree of order.

3. We live in a universe of connectedness, and we actually participate in the operation of it.

1. Our universe is a universe of Law. This is an orderly universe—from top to bottom and from inside to outside. For instance, we have already seen that although the very beginning of the universe (the Big Bang) may appear to have been chaotic, absolute order, balance and harmony underpinned everything. In fact, the chaos itself was necessary to the unfolding harmony. *The same, by the way, is often true in our own lives.*

Everything—EVERYTHING—we want to accomplish in our lives will always be done through the understanding and use of appropriate laws. Everything will be orderly, although it may not always feel that way. This is one of the most important keys to making miracles in our lives.

Here's an example. Gravity is probably the best known physical phenomenon, and for years, the idea of a "flying machine" was thought to be only fantasy. But, after many failed attempts, Orville and Wilbur Wright *did* construct a machine that flew—and then another that flew even greater distances.

The Wright brothers did not defy the law of gravity. They actually *worked with it.* Very simply, the velocity of the wind passing over the slightly curved top of the plane's wing was greater than that across the flat under-side. This lowered the downward pressure and caused an upward thrust of the plane. So their plane flew. New law? No. The law of gravity did not change. Aerodynamic principles did not change. Nothing changed except that *the Wright brothers developed a greater understanding and use of the existing laws and principles.*

Here's another application of the same law. If you throw a large piece of heavy metal into water, you'll find that it sinks. Why, then, does a metal cruise ship, weighing tens of tons, float? Why doesn't it sink? Different law?

No, simply a greater understanding of the principles related to the law of gravity.

This is an illustration of Archimedes Principle, which says that the weight of an object is counteracted by the weight of the volume of water it displaces. Because the ship is hollow, the steel cruise ship (even though it may weigh thousands of tons) actually weighs less than the water it displaces. Therefore, it floats. This is why a bottle with its top on will float in the dishpan, but when the top is removed and the bottle fills with water, it will sink.

The key point I'm making, of course, has nothing to do with airplanes or cruise ships or even Archimedes. The key point is this:

There are laws at work everywhere in our lives, and these natural (and spiritual) laws produce completely different results depending on how they are used.

2. Natural law is the physical expression of a *higher degree of order.* "As above, so below." (Remember this quote from page 6?) If you wish, you can call this higher degree of order "Spiritual law." The famous astrophysicist Sir James Jeans referred to this higher degree of order as "an Infinite Thinker thinking mathematically," and to the universe as looking "more like a great thought than like a great machine."[4] This is particularly significant because he was contrasting a consciousness-based universe with the mechanistic universe of Newtonian physics. This gives the unmistakable implication that a higher form of thought or Thinker is responsible for the universe and everything in it.

There is a Universal Power and Intelligence underpinning this awesome universe we inhabit. This is the same Power and Intelligence that underpins each one of us as we move through our lives.

So regardless of how you want to look at it or what you choose to call it, this higher degree of order, or Spiritual law, is reflected in everything that happens and in everything that is. And that includes you and me!

The Spiritual and mental laws and principles we discuss in later chapters are every bit as infallible and predictable as the laws of nature. Just as the Wright brothers were able to fly once they made the proper application of the principles of aerodynamics and the working of natural law, we, too, make "miracles" in our lives when we make the proper application(s) of Spiritual law.

However, we don't have to understand the laws and principles that govern our lives in order to use them. We are always using them whether we fully understand them or not. (Flying birds are a perfect example.) Each of us lived with and used the law of gravity long before we even *knew* there was such a thing as gravity. So, too, do we use the Spiritual laws and principles that govern our lives. All the time! Every day! 24/7!

The laws of the universe are always working, bringing either positive or negative results into our lives depending on how we're using them. (When the top is on the bottle, it floats, and when the top is off the bottle, it sinks. Same law, different application, different result.)

3. We live in a universe of connectedness, and we actually participate in the operation of it. From the time of the philosopher Plato and the mathematician Pythagoras, and even back to the ancient mysteries of Egypt, sages and philosophers have believed that we live in a universe of connectedness. But it was not until the twentieth century and the exploration of quantum physics that this was scientifically demonstrated.

Equally amazing, during the past forty years or so, science has begun to recognize and reveal one of the most important and exciting aspects of miracles:

Man's role in the universe is not that of an observer, but rather that of a participator.

John Wheeler, Ph.D., of Princeton University, sees this involvement of the observer as the most important feature of quantum theory and he has therefore suggested replacing the word "observer" with the word "participator."[5]

In other words:

Miracles don't happen to us, they happen by *means* of us.

Contrary to the popular belief that miracles are the random gifts of a whimsical deity, science today is demonstrating that we have an active role in the circumstances of our lives.

All of this is due to the comparatively recent scientific study of quantum physics—an Alice-in-Wonderland world where *nothing* seems to make any sense compared to how the world appears to our five senses. However, it is the place where Spiritual law begins its expression in the physical world by means of natural law.

ENTERING THE WORLD OF THE QUANTUM

The entry into the world of the quantum was accidental. As scientists probed deeper into the study of the universe, they were puzzled by findings that didn't make sense based on anything else they knew. And for a very long time after they first became able to study the behavior of particles at the quantum level, none of them knew quite what to make of their weird findings. The only consistency seemed to be that their findings were consistently bizarre and unpredictable—and that they, themselves, were consistently puzzled and frustrated. Their findings *were contradicting the basic tenets of classical (Newtonian) physics that had governed the world for the preceding 300 years!*

These great men with brilliant minds made comments such as these:

- Henri Poincaré, an exceptional French mathematician and physicist, when he unwittingly stumbled across a quantum effect that he realized could completely change the whole Newtonian model of the solar system:

> "These things are so bizarre that
> I cannot bear to contemplate them."[6]

- Albert Einstein, again objecting to what seemed to him an element of unpredictability or randomness in science:

> "God does not play dice."[7]

- Niels Bohr, a leading theoretical physicist who was among the pioneers in the study of the quantum world:

> "Anyone who is not shocked by quantum theory
> has not understood it."[8]

- Erwin Schroedinger, one of the founders of quantum theory:

> "I don't like it, and I'm sorry
> I ever had anything to do with it."[9]

What was taking place in the scientific world to provoke these amazing comments? What were these men finding that was so puzzling and shocking to them? As scientists probed the mysteries of quantum physics, these were some of the astonishing, puzzling and scientifically-confounding phenomena they encountered:

- As they searched to find elementary particles, they found, instead, "things" that actually changed form and properties as the particles responded to each other and to the scientists observing them!

- They found waves becoming particles... and particles becoming waves. Sometimes these "things" actually danced into and out of existence as they moved from the world of the invisible into the world of the visible... and back out again.

- As unbelievable as it sounds, these sub-atomic particles somehow even seemed to "know" what the observer was testing for—and they did it![10]

- Further, if the observer changed his/her mind about what he/she wanted to observe, the particle immediately responded to the new "desire" or "expectation" of the observer.[11]

These things were so astonishing because for over 500 years, from the time of Copernicus and Galileo, scientists had understood our world to operate like a perfect machine governed by exact mathematical laws. Man lived in it, used and enjoyed it, but was not "connected" to it in any way. Newtonian physics dealt with a world that was believed to be predictable, mechanistic and precise.

With the evolution of quantum physics, however, that changed.

Newton's theories are now recognized to apply to the visible world; however, they simply don't work at the sub-atomic level. Conversely, quantum theory is applicable at the level of both the visible (macroscopic) and invisible (sub-atomic) world.

Essentially, then, quantum theory does not *replace* Newtonian physics; it _transcends_ it by extending our scientific knowledge into the sub-atomic realm, a realm where the laws of physics are completely different.

Here are some of the main aspects of Newtonian physics, which now have been supplemented by a better understanding of our universe because of the "new science" of quantum physics.

According to Newtonian physics:

1. Our universe was believed to be an "objective universe." This meant:
   a. It was understood only through the five senses.
   b. Anything that had an impact on it was observable, measurable and predictable.
   c. Any influence we had on the universe was only through our actions.

2. Our universe was "deterministic" (predictable).

3. Anything real had to have visible and tangible form.

4. We lived in a world of material forms separated by "empty" space.

Through the study of the quantum realm, we now know that not one of the above statements is so. For example, science has now learned that:

1. We live in a universe that is "an undivided whole."

2. We are one with it, and part of it.

3. It is a world of potentiality rather than predictability.

4. We actually participate in the operation of this universe—it responds to us.

It took many years before physicists realized that the paradoxes they were encountering are *essential aspects of quantum physics.* They had to let go of their basic concepts, their language, their whole way of thinking—none of it was relevant to the quantum world. But when they *did* let go of the old paradigms and began asking the right questions, they were able to accurately formulate what we know today as "quantum theory," which I'll explain in a moment.

In the world of the quantum, science has found a world that is rich, complex and deeply intimate.

- Rather than a world of separateness, it has found a world of relationships.

- Rather than a world of "critical mass," it has found a world of "critical relationships."

- Rather than a world of predictability, it has found a world of potentialities.

- Rather than a world that is merely here for us to use and enjoy, it has found a world in whose operation we are active participants by the mere existence of our consciousness—a world responsive to our awareness of it and our mental interactivity with it!

This illustrates how important it is *to be able to open to new ways of thinking*. Scientists are trained to do this, but we too can do the same thing when we set, or determine, our intention, and commit to be open in our thinking.

HOW ENERGY FLOWS

In 1900, a young German student named Max Planck opened the door to the quantum realm when he wrote a formula on a postcard and mailed it to a colleague. In that formula, he theorized that energy was not absorbed and emitted in a steady stream, as was then believed, but rather that it was contained in separate little packets that he called "*quanta*." (The singular is "quantum," Latin for "packet.")

Another major advance took place in 1926, when Werner Heisenberg made an amazing discovery called "The Heisenberg Uncertainty Principle." It was this discovery that subsequently led to the development of *quantum theory*, or the theory of movement at the quantum level.

In the macrocosmic, or visible, world, particles are things, but in the quantum world, a particle is not a thing or an entity. A quantum particle is a "*tendency* to exist" or a "*tendency* to happen."

A quantum particle is a "potential" waiting to become something.

Additionally, a quantum particle actually has two forms of being—particle and wave. When the scientist measures its position, it becomes a particle, but when its movement is being measured, it becomes a wave. In other words, scientists learned they could measure either the particle aspect or the wave aspect—either location or movement—but could not measure both *at the same time*.

Based on this strange particle/wave phenomenon, Heisenberg formulated his now-famous "Uncertainty Principle," e.g., the more accurately you try to measure the position of a sub-atomic particle*, the less accurately you can measure its speed, and vice versa.

---

*At that time, there were only three known elementary particles: electrons, protons and neutrons. Today, science has identified over one hundred, with strange names such as "quark," "photon," "muon," "lepton" and "neutrino."

This principle led Heisenberg, together with Erwin Schroedinger and Paul Dirac, to develop the theory of quantum mechanics.

MORE DISCOVERIES AT THE QUANTUM LEVEL

Originally scientists thought there must be some unknown reason they weren't able to observe the well-defined positions and velocities of quantum particles. Finally, they realized quantum particles *didn't have* well-defined positions and velocities. Quantum theory said that these particles actually had a "quantum state" that was *a combination of both position and velocity.*

As they delved further into this strange realm, scientists learned they could make predictions when large numbers of sub-atomic occurrences were involved, but single sub-atomic events did not seem to have any relationship to the larger occurrences. Were these events simply random, or what? At the quantum level, cause and effect as scientists had always understood it simply did not seem to exist.

Scientists eventually learned that, in general, quantum physics does not predict a single definite result for any given observation quantum physics predicts *a number* of different potential outcomes, and tells us the likelihood of each of these.[12]

So, instead of working with the exact *predictability* they had experienced with Newtonian physics, scientists found themselves in the uncomfortable position of working with *possibilities* and *probabilities*. It was their worst nightmare come true!

It was too early for scientists to realize that these puzzling observations were the first glimmering of the fact that *the physical world responds to our expectations.* That recognition would not come for another half century.

It is exactly this area of "potential" and "probability" that opens the door to all the variety of manifestation at the physical level.

OUR WORLD OF UNBROKEN CONNECTEDNESS

all is ONE

It was actually in an effort to discredit quantum theory that Einstein accidentally established that the world in which we live is one in which there is an invisible connection between all things.

Despite his own Nobel-Prize-winning contribution to quantum theory, Einstein had remained very skeptical of this whole new field. The unpredictability of it all really bothered him. Something *had* to be wrong with the new theory.

During the mid-1930's, Einstein had many debates with his colleague and friend Niels Bohr, one of which related to whether or not matter could be affected by an influence that might travel faster than the speed of light.*
Quantum theory seemed to indicate that this could be so, but for years within the scientific community, "everybody knew" that nothing could travel faster than the speed of

---

*In scientific terms, this is known as "influence by a non-local cause."

light. It was one of the basic tenets of Einstein's own special theory of relativity!

Intending to discredit quantum theory, Einstein and two of his associates (Boris Podolsky and Nathan Rosen) put together a mathematical "thought exercise" that carried quantum theory to ridiculous lengths—and they arrived at what everybody agreed was an absolutely ridiculous answer.

First, some background:

Sub-atomic particles (electrons, for instance) have a property called "spin." When two electrons are "paired," they behave as a single unit. If one spins up, the other spins down; if one spins right, the other spins left. If the spin of one electron changes, the spin of the other electron changes direction as well—instantly.

This famous "thought exercise" became known as the EPR Paradox* and showed that according to quantum theory, this behavior would remain unchanged *regardless of how far apart the electrons were from each other.* One electron could be a half-world away from its twin, and it would respond *instantly* with the corresponding complementary spin. In other words, they would behave as one completely unified electron.

There were two "impossibles" with this proposal... or so thought the scientific community at the time. First,

*Named, of course, for Einstein, Podolsky and Rosen.

it would be impossible for one electron, many thousands of miles from its twin, to "know" that the spin of the other had changed. Secondly, even if there were some sort of long-distance communication, it would still be impossible for this electron to "know" and respond *instantly*. This would violate a limitation imposed by Einstein's special theory of relativity: Nothing travels faster than the speed of light. So, either quantum theory was wrong—or one of the tenets of Einstein's special theory of relativity was wrong. Debate raged long and heavy for the next thirty years... until it turned out *both are correct*.*

Unfortunately, Einstein didn't live long enough to see his EPR Paradox proven valid. He died in 1955, and it was another nine years before a physicist named John S. Bell developed what became known as "Bell's Theorem."* This theorem proved that Einstein's tongue-in-cheek proposition does, in fact, hold true: *Instantaneous change in widely-separated systems does take place.*

Henry Stapp, a physicist at Berkeley and probably the leading authority on the implications of Bell's Theorem, has called it, "The most important discovery in the history of science."[13]

What does all this mean? And how can it be understood without contradicting Einstein's important theory

---

*The reason both are correct is that while quantum theory (including the spin of widely-separated paired electrons) is valid at the level of both the macrocosm and the microcosm, Newtonian physics (including the speed of light) is applicable only to the macrocosm and, therefore, is not valid at the level of the quantum.

that nothing travels faster than the speed of light? Well, it means, very simply, that the two electrons—no matter how far apart they are—*are part of an indivisible whole that cannot be broken into parts.* There is no long-distance communication; *there is an invisible and unbroken connectedness.*

This was the first scientific proof of a web of connectedness between all things in the universe!

To this day science continues to prove that at the quantum level communication takes place—not at the speed of light, but *instantaneously.* Experiments have proved that just as the one particle "knew" when to change its spin to correspond with its twin, wave/particles in laboratory tests *even seem to "know" what kind of experiment was being conducted and to behave accordingly.*

For our purposes, possibly the most important experiment is known as the "double-slit experiment." (See Appendix A for a more complete description and scientific comments.) Very simply, if the observer is measuring motion, the wave/particles become waves; if the observer is measuring location, they obediently become particles. If the researcher changes the experiment at the last moment, the

---

*A theorem makes predictions and is "proven" when experimental results are consistent with those predictions. In the early 1970s, Bell's Theorem was experimentally confirmed by John Clauser at Berkeley, and since then, other experiments have consistently supported this important theorem.

wave/particle responds instantly. Repeatedly, science has found that particles and waves respond to the *expectation of the experimenter* and do what he/she wants them to do.

FIELDS

There is one final area of quantum physics that is important to cover: fields.

Despite the fact that for centuries, atoms were believed to be the fundamental building blocks of matter, science has now learned that the basic substance of the universe is comprised of invisible quantum (sub-atomic) fields.

A very simple definition of quantum fields would be:

Non-material patterns of energy that exert visible influence.

As an example, put some iron filings near a magnet and watch the patterns that form. These patterns are due to the invisible *magnetic field.* Other well-known fields are the *gravitational field* existing between physical bodies, and *electromagnetic fields,* such as those which radiate from radio and TV transmitter antennas.

Fields exist throughout space and time. They are the medium through which energy is carried in the form of waves. It is from these fields of energy that particles emerge.

The fields in the universe are infinite in number, and they are endlessly flowing, moving, being drawn toward or repelled from other fields.

Researchers such as Robert Jahn and Brenda Dunne of the Princeton Engineering Anomalies Research Laboratory[14] suggest that the realm of the mind, where thoughts are born, behaves much like the quantum realm of waves and particles. Let me try to explain very simply what this approach means to you and me—and miracles.

When electricity moves along a wire, it creates a field. So, too, when a thought moves in mind, it creates a field. When that field interacts with another field, something happens—a particle emerges. **An idea begins to take form.**

Although there remains much scientific work to be done:

Every step continues to scientifically verify the concept that the quantum realm is the transitional realm between Spirit and the material world—the realm where the Power, Intelligence, balance and harmony that created the universe continues to move into physical expression.

Even more exciting:

It is a realm that responds to the expectancy of the individual observer/ participant.

This is an all-important point. The meaning of these awesome new findings can best be summarized in the words of individual scientists themselves:

- British physicist David Bohm, "Ultimately, the entire universe (with all its 'particles,' including those constituting human beings, their laboratories, observing instruments, etc.) has to be understood as a single undivided whole."[15]

- Apollo 14 astronaut Edgar Mitchell, "Because the rules of quantum theory are supposed to apply to all matter, not just subatomic matter, by extension of this ubiquitous, interconnected 'resonance,' the suggestion is that all nature is in some sense wavelike, fieldlike and 'mindlike' in a way that isn't yet fully understood."[16]

Imagine! There is a resonance present everywhere in nature, interacting and "mindlike."

- John Wheeler, well-known physicist at Princeton: "May the universe in some strange way be 'brought into being' by the participation of those who participate.... The vital act is the act of participation. 'Participator is the incontrovertible new concept given by quantum mechanics.'"[17]

Does this mean that our consciousness directly affects the affairs of our lives in the "real" world? Does this mean that human consciousness actually shapes the mighty events of the universe itself?

The most profound statement on this comes, once more, from Henry Stapp, the authority on the implications of Bell's Theorem. Stapp contends that:

"Bell's Theorem demonstrates the effect of human consciousness at the level of the macroscopic."[18]

This means the world we *see*! This means therefore the world we live in can no longer be considered an "objective universe," or one which is separate from us.

Commenting on this statement by Stapp, author Dr. Larry Dossey writes, "The impact of our consciousness lies both in the direction of the very small and the very large. The sword of consciousness cuts both toward the galaxy and the atom."[19]

What is the impact of Dossey's words?

If the impact of our consciousness affects not only the very small (the microcosm) but also the very large (the macrocosm), then it must also affect each of us and the very events of our lives. If this is so, we need to be very clear in our understanding of consciousness—and, even more importantly, in how we use it.

So, although there remains a great deal of scientific work to fully substantiate and explain exactly how the invisible moves into the visible in our lives, we do know that the potentiality with which the invisible first makes itself known is directly affected by consciousness—our consciousness.

This is where you come in.

PART TWO

WHERE YOU FIT IN

There is one mind common to all individual men. Every man is an inlet to the same and to all of the same.

— RALPH WALDO EMERSON —

CHAPTER 4

ENTER... YOU, THE THINKER

NOW we come to the most important person in your world—you!

And, indeed, if you do not already consider yourself the most important person in your world, I hope you will change your mind by the time you finish reading this chapter.

You are the observer or "participator" in your world. In terms of miracles, what this means is simply this:

- You are the thinker in your life.
- You are the participator in your world.
- You are the co-creator of the things that happen to you.

We learned in the last chapter that we actually participate in the things that take place at the level of the quantum, and, subsequently, in the things that take place in our world. But exactly *how* do we participate? In one way, and one way only: *At the level of consciousness.*

Remember the all-important Law of Co-Creation:

**Consciousness manifests.
Dominant thought prevails.**

In the last chapter, we explored this from the scientific point of view.

Thought is energy. And it is the interaction of the energy of thought with another form of energy—in this case, the quantum—that directs the quantum to make the change from unexpressed potentiality to expressed actuality.

So, in some strange way that scientists have observed but do not yet fully understand, our consciousness affects the quantum in the process of its expression. This tells us:

**What we choose to think is of primary importance
in terms of what happens in our world.**

Also important is the recognition that this creative principle works whether or not we understand it. Just as the law of gravity is always working and we are always using it whether or not we understand it, the same is true of creative principles: They are always at work, and we are always using them whether or not we understand them. *When we know that such principles exist, however, and we learn to work with them and use them properly, we begin to make miracles in our lives.*

You see, miracles don't come about by chance. They don't come about because we're nice people. They also don't come about just because we want them desperately (although it does help to *really* want your miracle). Miracles come about because of consciousness.

**It is through our consciousness
that we create the miracle(s).**

And because of this, we are not victims.

**Miracles are the spiritual birthright
of each one of us.**

If our consciousness is the primary determinant of our miracle or the good we want in our world, then let's get clear on what *consciousness* is. Although *Webster's Dictionary* defines "consciousness" as "mental awareness," this is a very incomplete definition.

Our consciousness is the entire mental field encompassing all the intentions, thoughts, feelings, emotions and experiences (waking and sleeping, conscious and subconscious) that we have ever had or experienced.

Thus our mind and our brain are two different things. Our brain is the physical receptor and storage unit of all our experiences, and our mind is the initiator—"the thinker," as it were. Our brain operates at the level of the visible; our mind, the invisible. So when we talk about consciousness, we are talking not about the brain but about our individual mind.

All that we ever are, ever have been, or ever will be conscious of comes only through our mind. And all of that will always remain part of our consciousness.

THE CONSCIOUS MIND, THE SUBJECTIVE MIND, AND UNIVERSAL CREATIVE POWER

Although we have one *and only one* mind and it is indivisible, it functions at two very different levels, identified as follows:

1. Our conscious mind (also known as the "surface" mind or the "objective mind")

2. Our subjective mind (also known as the "deeper" mind or the "subconscious" mind)

The conscious mind:

- Is the mind of the five senses.
- Receives all our information from the outer world.

- Is what we use to reason, analyze, discern, judge and make decisions.
- Very importantly, with our conscious mind we choose:

  a. What we want to think.
  b. What we want to be.
  c. What we want to do.
  d. What we want to have.

Our subjective* (or subconscious) mind:

- Receives and retains everything we think, say, do and experience.
- Accepts as true everything that comes to it through the conscious mind, provided that the conscious mind accepts it as true.
- Does not judge the thought patterns coming to it from the conscious mind. It simply goes about bringing into our lives experiences and conditions that are congruent with our dominant beliefs.
- Changes only in accordance with the thoughts entertained in our conscious mind.
- Is characterized by absolute obedience to what it receives.

---

*"Subjective" and "subconscious" mind are interchangeable, but I prefer "subjective" because this more clearly connotes that this part of our mind is subject to the input of the conscious mind.

- Is our connection with the unlimited Universal Mind, or Creative Force of the universe.*

Essentially, then:

Our conscious mind is the choosing, selecting, initiating phase of our mind.

Our subjective mind is the deep, active, producing phase of our mind and is linked to the Universal Creative Force and Intelligence.

At this point, it becomes easier to see why author Dr. Deepak Chopra refers to the quantum realm as the transitional realm between Spirit and the material world, for the quantum moves into and out of existence between the material world and the world of the Absolute—the world of Spirit, God, Source, First Cause.

The Absolute realm of Spirit is the realm of Unconditional Love, Infinite Wisdom, Absolute Power and Perfect Peace. It is the realm beyond space and time. It is changeless. It is eternal.

---

*The relationship between subjective mind and the Universal Creative Power (Universal Mind, God, Infinite Intelligence, Absolute Power) is brilliantly detailed by Judge Thomas Troward in *The Edinburgh Lectures* and *The Creative Process and the Individual.* Although they were written over 100 years ago, these books remain the standard by which similar books addressing this profound subject are judged. Professor William James of Harvard said of these books, "Far and away the ablest statement of that philosophy that I have met...."

It is the energy of the dominant thought in our subjective mind that creates the influence that then begins the process of manifestation in this world.

"Thought" can be either an individual thought or many thoughts. Whenever we speak of "dominant thought," we are talking about the dominant *field* of thought or the dominant pattern of thinking in our consciousness. It is comprised of a great deal of similar thinking, amplified by the emotional intensity of the thinking.

Our dominant patterns of thinking become a conduit for the flow of the Creative Power of the Universe.

Contrary to what many people believe, our subjective mind does not "judge" the directions it gets from the conscious mind. This is how it works:

1. What we entertain in our conscious mind goes into our subjective mind.

2. Our subjective mind accepts, without question and without judgment, whatever thoughts we give to it.

3. Our subjective mind is one with the Creative Force of the Universe. Through the interaction of our subjective mind and the quantum, this Creative Force brings into expression in our

world the dominant desires, thoughts and beliefs held in our subjective mind.

Indeed, the universe's hidden laws are expressions of the creative process, as Love, Power, Intelligence and the Harmony of Spirit move into expression in our physical world in response to our thinking.

So, what happens in our world is not random, after all.

To the extent that we can open to It and accept It, the Love, Intelligence and Power that created the awesome universe that we live in is available to us—to bring healing into our lives, balance and harmony into our relationships, prosperity into our world and creative direction in everything we do.

Our subjective mind isn't the only thing that makes no judgment.

The Creative Force makes no judgment. It simply responds to whatever demand is placed on it by our subjective mind.

In other words, It does not decide that the negative attitudes we are expressing might not reflect what we *really* want in our lives. Its singular response is to say "Yes" to our dominant thoughts and beliefs—to bring them into manifestation.

Simple, right? Yes, very simple. So, then, where's the rub? The rub is that our subjective mind receives *all* the thoughts, experiences and reactions that have *ever* been in our conscious mind—and much of that is negative. Although we may not realize it, the dominant thoughts contained in our subjective mind are often far more negative than we imagine. So, what we experience in our lives is often far more negative than we want, and, in many cases, our lives themselves are far more negative and unrewarding than we want.

The beauty that can be found here, however, is this:

When we understand how the creative laws work, we can then begin using them correctly to change the things in our lives that aren't working for us.

We can transform negative thought patterns into thought patterns that will bring into our world whatever good we are looking for—miracles—so that we have a more joyous and fulfilling life. Therefore, it stands to reason:

**Your mind—your consciousness—
is your greatest asset.**

It is the key to your miracle(s). Learning how to properly use your mind is the shortcut to your miracle and to all the miracles that follow. In a manner of speaking, the proper use of your mind provides the tunnel through the mountain.

Remember our definition of a miracle:

A miracle is a series of natural events occurring in the right sequence, and at the right time, to produce wonderful results.

By now, it is probably easier to understand why miracles are a "series of natural events." They are governed by the same natural process that produces all the events in our lives.

When we learn how to use natural laws they serve us well. When we misuse them or use them with limited understanding, we get either unfavorable or limited results. This is true of natural law as well. Think for a moment of what happens if you turn on the electrical switch of a lamp (favorable) as contrasted to what happens if you stick your finger into an electrical outlet (not too favorable). This means:

Good and bad results come from *different applications of the same law.* The creative laws, like all laws, are completely impersonal.

Many people spend most of their lives believing that they cannot break free of the life they are currently living. They believe they cannot heal physically, they cannot be successful, or they cannot be prosperous. None of this is true.

No matter who you are and no matter how bad your life may be at this moment, the proper use of these laws will bring positive changes into your world.

THE CO-CREATIVE PROCESS

Although the co-creative process is one continuous, ever-present action, it can be understood in three main aspects:

- The Law of Belief
- The Law of Expectancy
- The Law of Attraction

The first two are very inter-related, and the third is the result of Universal Intelligence and Power responding to the first two. We set the creative process in motion through the Law of Belief and the Law of Expectancy. Then, the Law of Attraction takes over.

THE LAW OF BELIEF

"What you believe, you will receive; what you doubt, you will live without." This is a rephrasing of the Hermetic teaching, "As above, so below; as within, so without."

Each of us has a whole set of beliefs about ourselves and our lives. All together, this set of beliefs constitutes our personal Law of Belief.

And the Law of Belief operates two ways.

1. It is always in the process of formation, being influenced by everything we think, hear, say and experience.

2. It is always producing in our lives those things that are congruent and commensurate with itself.

Our belief system is so powerful that it is the foundation for our lives today—whatever that may be. Now, if your life is not all that you would like it to be, this may be a little hard to accept. But remember that you're not alone. *All of us* have areas of our lives that we want to improve. We're *all* growing. Besides, it's wonderful to know that if our belief system played a big part in our being where we are, then we are not powerless when it comes to making changes for the better.

Think about what this really means. It means that we do not have to be a victim of circumstances.

We don't have to be a victim of anything.

We don't have to go through life letting life "happen" to us. We can move through life choosing the kind of life we want and actually having it unfold in our world.

This process sounds very simple, doesn't it? Well, if it's so simple, why isn't everybody making miracles in their lives? First, as we discussed, not everybody knows and understands the hidden laws of the universe. But, second:

Most of us are unaware that some (or even many) of our beliefs may be limiting. We don't recognize our negative thinking, or if we do, we often have no idea of the extent to which we engage in it.

Can you imagine what it would be like if Life responded immediately every time you thought to yourself, "I am so embarrassed, I could almost die," or, "I'd give my right arm to have a job like that!"?

But if our subjective mind takes literally everything we think and say, and if it immediately goes to work to bring these things into existence in our lives, why *don't* they all happen, negative thoughts and all? Because our consciousness is comprised of *all* our mental experiences, and it is our *dominant thought* about something that manifests in the dominant pattern of our lives.

It takes repeated and consistent thought on our part to change a negative dominant thought pattern to one that is positive.

As our belief system is based on what we believe to be true, changing it does not come about easily. Think for a moment about the last time you disagreed with someone about some "fact"—or even about an opinion. Isn't it true we spend much of our time mentally and verbally defending our positions on everything from big things to little things—from what to do about air pollution to which way to cut our food?

Whenever we encounter new information that conflicts with our established beliefs, our first reaction is to attack or dismiss the new information in order to maintain the integrity of the old—just as Einstein did with Willem de Sitter and Aleksander Friedmann. We all do it. We mentally "argue" our position and further reinforce our thinking. Having done this, we continue to recreate the same types of experiences with different people and places. This is why the lives of so many of us seem like re-runs with a changing cast of characters.

It's generally this way every time someone or something challenges our current belief system. We use that experience to consciously reinforce our beliefs. We don't like to be wrong.

It is only when we truly change our thinking that we change our consciousness, and when we change our consciousness our world changes automatically. This is what is meant by the phrase, "consciousness manifests." The dominant beliefs and thoughts in our consciousness *manifest in our world.*

Of course, our belief system can be positive and healthy in certain areas and at the same time limiting in others. For example, we may enjoy wonderful health but at the same time have great difficulty financially. Or, we may enjoy wonderful professional success in our lives but encounter serious and consistent relationship problems. How did the differences develop?

HOW DID OUR PERSONAL BELIEF SYSTEM DEVELOP?

Our belief system grows almost like an inverse pyramid based largely on just a few core beliefs about our lives and ourselves. These core beliefs may not be things that we figured out for ourselves—rather, they usually are things we learned in childhood about ourselves and about what we could expect from the world. We learn from our parents how to respond to the world. Is it friendly? Is it safe? Is it fair? Is it good? Bad? Dangerous?

Even more importantly—are *we* okay? Or is there something "not okay" about us? Are we *valuable?*

We also learned from our childhood families how to regard ourselves in relationship *to others.* Are we better than our relatives and neighbors? Or, are they better than we are? Do we have to work hard for everything, or does it come easily? Are we stronger than or weaker than they are? More handsome or more homely? Smarter or not as smart?

Our beliefs cause us to see the world in a way *that is unique to each of us.* This is our individual paradigm—the way we see things. One person lives life freely and with a cheerful and open manner that expects and invites trust and reliability whereas the next person lives from a standpoint of great fear and concern that others are "out to get you." One person moves forward with great confidence and self-assurance while another is timid and uncertain.

People raised in financial comfort are likely to live with an expectancy of financial abundance in anything they do, while those raised in poverty are likely to expect a life of hardship.

 The way we see the world is the way the world responds to us.

- Our programming and our conditioning lead to our beliefs.
- Our beliefs lead to our attitudes and our thoughts.
- Our attitudes and thoughts lead to our feelings.
- Our feelings determine how we think, act and behave.
- How we think, act and behave reinforces our beliefs, which in turn reinforce our attitudes which lead to our thoughts, and on and on.[1]

Our belief system is multifaceted. It covers just about anything and everything that we experience—although the four major areas in which we all either flourish or struggle are health, prosperity, relationships and success. So it is usually in these four areas that we look for our miracles.

As we have new experiences, we incorporate these into our belief system as part of what we know to be true about our lives and ourselves. Our belief system is built on a constantly growing body of experiences with circumstances and people, and is continually reinforced every time it is challenged.

OUR BELIEFS ABOUT OURSELVES

As children, all too often we come to believe at some very deep level that we are not "good enough," or we may not be "worthy" or are in some way personally inadequate. In too many cases, far too little of our childhood programming is positive and far too much is negative.

Let's take an example of a family where the programming is negative or critical. The oldest child may feel overburdened with responsibility; the middle one may feel overlooked and forgotten; and the youngest may feel that they are the recipient of hand-me-downs and odious comparisons. In each of these cases, the perception each child has about how they are treated will have a profound effect on how they view themselves as an adult. This perception leads each of them to the dominant thought they have of themselves. Interestingly:

In all three situations, each will grow up with some feeling of victimization.

Compare this with a family in which the oldest grows up feeling respected and privileged because he/she is older; the middle child gets extra guidance and protection from the older sibling; and the youngest is cherished by everyone as the precious "last gift" to the family. Here we will find three completely different sets of core beliefs, and:

All three children will feel valued and worthwhile.

The positive and respectful words and attitudes of parents have a profound effect on their children—and so do their negative and critical words and attitudes. A positive sense of self serves us well, but a negative one will sabotage us in many areas unless and until we are able to recognize this and make changes.

Psychologists know that many, if not most, people have deeply hidden feelings of insecurity and/or unworthiness about themselves. Dr. Maxwell Maltz was a pioneer in this field, and in his classic book *Psycho-cybernetics* he shares the amazing insights he gained from working with plastic surgery on countless patients. He learned that many people had very poor self-images based, he and they thought, on some physical disfigurement or something about their appearance that could be surgically corrected. Yet, he found that for many patients, their poor self-image remained completely unchanged after the surgical correction.[2]

Somewhere in their formative years, these people had been given the impression that they were not attractive and worthwhile. This became their "law of belief" about themselves—a belief they had probably reinforced every time they looked in a mirror and didn't like what they saw. So even after surgery to improve their outer appearance, they continued to see themselves as "flawed," "different" or "unattractive." It was as though they saw themselves through different eyes—and, indeed, they did.

Outwardly, they had changed, but their inner belief system did not change—and neither the mirror nor family and friends could tell them differently.

A "core belief" is usually something we accept without question at an early age. Thereafter, it continues to be reinforced by our observations and perceptions of our experiences. From that point on, the experiences in our lives serve to expand and reinforce this image, whether or not it's positive, whether or not it's negative, and whether or not it's accurate.

If the core belief is negative, it can be called a "limited" or "limiting" belief since it sets limits on what we can be, do, have or experience.

It is essential to change limited beliefs if we want to bring good things into our world.

When we change our consciousness, we replace limited beliefs with those that allow us to live fully expressed lives—beliefs that allow miracles to occur.

Life does not place limitations on us. Life is always ready to express fully and completely. The only limitations are those that we ourselves place on life, whether we intend to do so or not.

Our personal belief system leads to the second law.

THE LAW OF EXPECTANCY

The Law of Expectancy is what we expect—*truly expect*—to have happen in any given situation. When we expect something, we look forward to it with a very high degree of certainty, anticipation and maybe even excitement. We know that in all likelihood it will occur in the time and manner of our mental expectation.

Many of our beliefs may be so buried in our subjective mind that we may not even be in touch with them. Expectancy, however, is primarily in our conscious mind and, thus, much easier to alter. We can *choose* to change it because we are consciously in touch with it and have control over it.

We can control the thoughts we choose to entertain in our conscious mind.

As we consciously change our expectancy, we change what happens in our world and, at the same time, we gradually change our belief.

Whenever a miracle occurs, there has been a change in our belief, a change in consciousness, a change in the way we think about ourselves and the universe we inhabit.

We often hear that someone has had a "miraculous recovery." What really happened? Was it something supernatural, or was it a wonderfully natural occurrence?

To make the answer clear: Those who are healed in the waters of the world-famous healing shrine in Lourdes go there with a deep, subjective expectancy of healing, for if it were the water alone that was responsible for the miracle, everyone who went there would be healed. (Remember that *a law* works the same way, *all the time.* And it always works the same way *for everyone.*)

Truly, I know of countless "miraculous recoveries," and doctors will, on occasion, even agree that a miracle has happened. In all too many cases, however, they shake their heads, puzzled, and either say they "just don't understand it" or else suggest that their original diagnosis may have been in error.

A memorable example of this took place about four years ago. An eleven-year-old girl named Robin was involved in a horrific automobile accident. The three people in the other car were killed, while Robin was the only one injured in the car in which she was riding. Her spinal cord was severed and, as a result, she was paralyzed from the waist down. Additionally, the sharp force of the seat belt during the impact caused terrible damage to her abdominal organs.

Robin's internal injuries were severe, and she had lost an enormous amount of blood. At the hospital in Ann Arbor, Michigan, surgeons performed immediate trauma surgery on her kidney, spleen and colon. (As she was a terrific athlete and dancer, doctors said later that her youth and physical strength had helped her survive.)

Forty-eight hours later, doctors performed still another essential surgery, one that involved the spinal fusion of two steel rods to support her severed spinal column.

About ten days later, Robin's primary doctor went to her mother, Virginia, with a disturbing request. As gently as possible, he said, "We need to check to see if Robin has an aneurysm in her abdomen." He explained that during his examinations over each of the last three days, he had detected a strong "swooshing" sound that usually indicated an aneurysm. He had waited three days to make sure he wasn't mistaken. While aneurysms were uncommon in children, he explained, it was very possible that the force of the seat belt might have caused an aneurysm when her body jack-knifed in the car.

Virginia told me later that at that moment, she felt certain that her beautiful young daughter, fighting bravely for life, could not survive another surgery. She felt pure terror as she thought of it. But then she began to shake her head. "No!" she said to herself. "I do not accept this. I see my child whole, and healthy. Some way, somehow, *there is no aneurysm.*"

From that moment, Virginia, who was a strong believer in spiritual healing, began to affirm Robin's wholeness. Constantly and consistently, whenever fearful thoughts came into her mind, she refused to entertain them. Instead, she would visualize the doctor telling her there was no aneurysm. No matter how it seemed, Virginia remembered an important axiom:

> **Think only about what you want, not about what you don't want.**

The MRI to find the aneurysm was done the same day. The following morning, the chief of vascular surgery met with both parents. With great gentleness, compassion and sadness, the doctor showed them the MRI and pointed out the aneurysm. He took a piece of paper (which Virginia still has) and drew a diagram to illustrate exactly where it was in Robin's lower abdomen. "This will not go away," he said. "It needs to be surgically corrected." The surgeon advised not waiting too long because the aneurysm could pop open from very little pressure.

Virginia was shocked. She had been so *very* certain—absolutely convinced, in fact—that the MRI would not show an aneurysm. Later, in her room, she sat quietly thinking about all that had happened. She didn't even know how to direct her thoughts, how to direct her prayers. Then it came to her, "Pray that no surgery is necessary.'" This she began to do.

Despite all medical indications to the contrary, Virginia would not allow herself to be disheartened, and she continued to entertain only thoughts and mental images that supported what she wanted.

Any time she thought about the aneurysm, Virginia would visualize the doctor telling her that no surgery would be necessary.

Virginia and her husband then decided to move Robin to the Rehabilitation Institute of Chicago for additional therapy so she would be closer to her family. Before Robin's therapy there could begin, however, the Institute told Virginia the aneurysm had to be corrected. Well, so be it. Virginia's family made the move, and then it was time for the surgery.

A follow-up MRI was taken first, however, and Virginia waited for the results. She kept visualizing the doctor telling her, "There is no aneurysm," and, "There will be no surgery." One day passed, then two, then three. Finally, two weeks went by, and *still* no word about the surgery. Virginia steeled herself and cornered the doctor. "What about the aneurysm?" she asked. There was a long pause. "Well," he finally said, "it's a funny thing, but the follow-up MRI doesn't show any aneurysm, so there won't be any surgery."

Virginia breathed, "Oh, it's a miracle." But the doctor corrected her, "No, it was simply not a real aneurysm. It was a pseudo-aneurysm." What was the difference? The doctor explained that a real aneurysm had a "strong swooshing sound" and "does not go away." Virginia smiled to herself as she walked away. She didn't bother to tell him about the three days of strong "swooshing" the doctors had heard in Ann Arbor. It didn't matter. The only important thing was that *her miracle had occurred.*

This story illustrates another important point about miracles:

> **We can bring about miracles in the lives of our loved ones.**

Virginia believed in miracles, and, contrary to all medical opinion and information, she kept her thoughts focused on what she wanted and not on what she didn't want.

- When we change our outlook, we change our consciousness.
- When we change our consciousness, things in our lives change automatically.

When we change our outlook on life, life changes for us. This is "life responding to the observer."

We live in a universe of infinite potential —and this potentiality is never limited by past experience.

What this means is that your miracle is not limited by the fact that "it's never happened before." The axiom here is:

Principle knows no precedent.

Isn't that a wonderful thing—to know that just because something hasn't happened before doesn't mean that it can't happen now. It *can* happen now! This is a universe of infinite good, capable of constantly producing infinitely new experiences. And each of us is in direct contact with this through the power of our subjective mind.

But, in order to experience this good, first we have to believe we are worthy of it, and second, we have to expect it.

There is absolutely no limit to the number of positive things that can happen in our lives—to every one of us!

THE LAW OF ATTRACTION

Once we do our part with the Law of Belief and the Law of Expectancy, the Law of Attraction immediately and automatically comes into operation. This last aspect of the creative process begins to unfold once the first two laws are invoked. Whatever we believe, whatever we expect, begins to be attracted into our life. *This is what determines the make-up of our present lives.*

The Law of Attraction works like a magnet. It brings into our lives the right people, the right situations and the right information to make our lives either good or bad. Those things that seem so serendipitous are the *normal operation* of the Law of Attraction. This is why the miraculous things that happen in our lives seem so natural as they're unfolding: They *are* natural!

Several years ago, I was counseling a man named Tom who owned a small electronics supply company. Although Tom was a good businessman, his firm was experiencing a serious financial challenge. A series of setbacks had left the company strapped financially. Their suppliers had cut his firm off, but now, after a lot of effort, everything was in place for a major turnaround.

Tom was excited and happy about the expected rebound, but he needed $40,000 to clear up past-due payments to the suppliers before they would ship to him. Yet everything Tom owned was tied up in this company; he had no other personal assets to draw on or to pledge. His bank had turned him down for a loan, and other banks and lending institutions had also turned him down. For some weeks, he and I together had been affirming the success of his business. Now, it seemed so close—but regardless of what Tom did or whom he contacted, he couldn't raise the $40,000. Without it, he stood to lose everything.

One Friday morning, Tom literally bounded into my office. He was beaming as he sat down. "I've located a new lending company," he said. "They know the whole story from A to Z and have virtually committed to the loan." He had all his financial papers in his briefcase in preparation for an eleven o'clock appointment the same day to draw up, and possibly even sign, the closing papers. This meant he would have the $40,000 he needed by the following week. Throughout our conversation, he kept repeating, "I know this is done. I simply know this is a done deal." Tom was one very happy man when he left my office. So was I.

I didn't hear from Tom again until Tuesday afternoon, and his story was truly astonishing. When it came time for his appointment to finalize arrangements for the loan, Tom was met with bad news. For some reason, the lending company had changed its mind. If his had been a new company, they said, they could offer the loan, but his was an established business, and the only funds they had available just then could be loaned only to new businesses. No matter what Tom said, there was nothing they could do to help him. They had no suggestions. Tom was in a state of shock.

Slowly, he walked back to the bank of elevators, pushed the "down" button, and, in a daze, got on the elevator.

Have you ever mistakenly gotten on an elevator going the wrong way? Well, that's what Tom did. In his confusion and despair, he simply got on the first elevator that came along—and it was going up.

Have you ever pushed one button after another trying to get off an elevator going the wrong way? Well, Tom did that, too. He finally managed to get the elevator to stop, and, gratefully, got off.

Again, he waited for an elevator. Just as it arrived, another businessman came running down the hall to jump in. Tom didn't even bother to look up at the person, so he was startled to hear his name. "Tom?" asked the new arrival. "Is that you?"

Tom looked up, puzzled for a moment, but then he recognized a high school buddy he hadn't seen in over twenty years. He brightened as much as he could, and the two shook hands. "How do you happen to be in this building?" asked Tom's friend. Briefly, Tom explained what had just taken place. When he finished, his chum said, "Come on. We need to go back up to my office."

When Tom called me on Tuesday afternoon, he had just finished depositing $40,000 into his company's account. Incredibly, it turned out that his high school buddy had been in the lending business for many years. Since Tom had all his financial papers with him, they were able to complete the application papers on the spot, and the funds were ready two business days later.

His business has flourished from that day to this.

Tom believed in himself and his company, and he had continued to expect his "miracle."

Although it didn't come through the channel he thought it would, the Law of Attraction drew him together with the right person at the right time. How serendipitous that Tom would "accidentally" get on the "wrong" elevator and run into just the "right" person to make the loan that would save his company.

If we want miracles, we need to make certain the energy of our thought is always congruent with what we want and not with what we don't want.

If we want to change our lives—if we want miracles in our lives—we need to change our expectancy, and to do that we need to change our belief system, and to do that, we need to change our thinking.

Now it's time to talk about exactly that: How we go about changing our thinking and *keeping* it changed!

CHAPTER 5

WHAT DO YOU THINK?

IF we want to change our thinking, it only makes sense that the first thing we have to do is to get a handle on what and how we currently think.

Someone once wrote,

> "If I think the same as I always thought,
> Then I'll get the same as I always got."

And now you know why!

Think of it this way. Suppose there were two piles of coins, with every coin of equal weight. And every morning suppose you could take as many coins as you wanted from either or both of the two piles—enough coins to fill one big bag. Then, suppose you learned that one pile contained nothing but gold coins (redeemable only for what you wanted) and the other pile contained nothing but lead coins (redeemable only for what you didn't want). Which would you take? You'd take the gold coins of course (or at least as many as you could fit into the bag!).

And so it is with our thoughts. Our positive thoughts are gold, redeemable only for what we want. Our negative thoughts are lead, redeemable only for what we don't want. But, most of us simply entertain whatever thoughts come into our minds without ever bothering to realize that they are, indeed, forming our world of tomorrow. They are either helping to establish or helping to prevent miracles from taking place in our lives.

It's time to make some changes that will lay the groundwork for a consciousness that truly produces miracles. Let's explore how to clear out some habitual ways of thinking that are negative—those speed bumps that slow down the process of bringing about a miracle.

I can almost hear you saying to yourself, "But I *am* a positive thinker!" And you may well be. But let's be sure. Because, if our thinking co-creates the circumstances of our lives, then we need to know and respect this axiom:

**All thought is creative—
negative thought as well as positive thought.**

Today, it's become almost fashionable to be, or at least to think of oneself as being, a positive thinker. In the course of my lifetime, only a handful of people have ever acknowledged to me that they were not positive thinkers—and even those few would add, "But, I *try* to be positive."

"Try" is a nice, positive-sounding word
that actually conceals a negative expectation.

For example, imagine that you invite two people to a party Friday evening and one says, "Oh, yes! I'd love to come. I'll be there," and the other says, "Oh, thank you. I'll *try* to make it." The second person has just laid the groundwork in your mind *and theirs* for not showing up. Now, this may be okay when you're talking about a Friday night party, but it's not okay when you're talking about changing your life—or making miracles.

The late, great Vince Lombardi was clear about this when he said of his Green Bay Packers, "When my boys go out on that football field, they don't go out to *try* to win. They go out *to win!*" And that's what we want to do. We want to *make* miracles. We don't want to *try* to make miracles.

So, don't decide to "try" to change your thinking from negative to positive. Decide to *do* it. By the way, "hope" is another positive-sounding word that usually covers up a negative expectation. (Think about it.)

So, you get to decide—and you can do it right now. You can "hope" for your miracle and decide to "try" to do the things necessary to have it happen; or you can decide to *expect* your miracle and *do your part* to let that miracle unfold in your world.

Remember, our beliefs and our expectations initiate the creative process that creates our conditions and circumstances, and it is our early beliefs that form the basis for future, related beliefs. They become increasingly interdependent and mutually supportive because when a conflicting idea presents itself, we tend to resolve the conflict in favor of the early, primary beliefs we learned when we were young.

This means that unless we consciously work to examine it, our network of individual beliefs continues to get stronger and stronger regardless of whether or not it is in alignment with what we want in our lives.

Think about this for a moment. Following the world-changing events of September 11, 2001, Americans across the country handled their personal lives and decisions in a variety of ways. Some people (many, in fact) refused to fly; others flew if they had no alternative; still others flew comfortably, giving virtually no thought to danger. Many canceled overseas travel plans; others followed through with theirs; and still others scheduled trips, delighted at the lack of crowding and lower prices they encountered. Some became aggressive in the stock market; others sold their holdings and put the funds in money-market accounts. Some people were tentative about making any future plans and would add as a precaution, "provided nothing else happens" (with "nothing else" being a reference to more terrorist attacks). In larger cities, Middle Eastern cab drivers reported that many fares were cold and even insulting; other passengers held out a hand of warmth and friendship, compassionately understanding the pain and embarrassment the driver might be experiencing. Without getting caught up in individual specifics, the variety of responses obviously did not depend on facts and circumstances because these were essentially the same for all of us. The responses depended on *each individual person and reflected their individual basic beliefs.* Additionally, the actions taken by each person also served to further reinforce a deeply-held core belief of each person, whatever it was. Interestingly, the core belief involved was essentially the same for each person: How safe is this universe for me? How safe is my world? Just think about all the ways each of our lives is affected *every day* by our individual answers to these very questions.

Most of us recognize that we have a running conversation going on with ourselves almost all the time. What we may not know is that this very conversation, this inner chatter or "self-talk," is pounding our belief system into place moment by moment, word by word.

Of our tens of thousands of thoughts each day, psychologists tell us that over 90% of them are the same things we thought the day before!

> We not only think the same thoughts about the same things over and over, but we also think the same *kinds* of thoughts about different things.

As a general rule, we are routinely open or closed to new ideas and suggestions; we are routinely spontaneous or not spontaneous; we can immediately see the humor in a situation, or we're pretty dour about it.

When you get to know someone quite well, can't you predict with some certainty how they're going to react to a given situation—or the type of thing they're going to say? Of course you can.

In both behavior and words, our reactions are the result of our beliefs, and our beliefs are the result of programming and consistent patterns of thought.

HOW TO CHANGE NEGATIVE THOUGHT PATTERNS

Important work in this area has been done in studies involving what is known as "cognitive therapy," a type of therapy that looks at how thoughts affect you emotionally, and helps you learn how to change your negative thought patterns. Although most of this work has been done with patients suffering from depression, the principles can benefit all of us.

Clinical depression affects millions of people and is one of our major health problems today. It is considered to be a medical illness and is generally accompanied by a change in brain chemistry. Traditional treatment has been to prescribe antidepressant medication either with or without psychotherapy.

In 1980, David D. Burns, M. D., published a revolutionary book called *Feeling Good: The New Mood Therapy*. It was the first public introduction to what is called "cognitive therapy," and Burns intended his book merely as a self-help supplement to traditional treatment for depression and anxiety. To the great surprise of everyone, tests during the following twenty years (done by medical researchers *other* than Burns) demonstrated that not only was cognitive therapy at least as effective as drugs in treating depression, but for many patients, it was even *more* effective.[1]

Medical science determined that changes in brain chemistry occurred in patients using medication, but:

> Astonishingly, they found that changes in brain chemistry also took place with patients using only cognitive therapy.[2]

How does this apply to miracles? The first principle of cognitive therapy is that all of our moods and emotions are created by our thoughts. Essentially, a "cognition" is the way we look at things–our perceptions, mental attitudes and beliefs. It includes not only the way we interpret things but also what we say to ourselves about a given situation or person—in other words, our inner dialogue.

In cognitive therapy, the patient learns to recognize consistent thought patterns that are actually negative exaggerations of existing circumstances. For example, a salesman who loses a customer may begin mentally berating himself, saying to himself something like, "I'm a real loser. I can't do anything right. I'll never amount to anything." This harsh and illogical self-criticism soon becomes automatic.

In cognitive therapy, the depressed person learns to address and correct this type of thinking with something more realistic and appropriate. The salesman might correct the above by saying, "I do a lot of things right! I am a winner, and losing one account is nothing more than a challenge I faced today. I'll simply have to examine what I might have done differently to save this account and use this whole thing as a learning experience."

So, as this person learns to correct the negative exaggeration in their thinking, their dominant thought gradually shifts from negative to positive—and after a while, the automatic negative reactions become progressively less powerful and less consistent. As this happens, the person's depression begins to lift and their brain chemistry begins to normalize.

This is exactly what we are talking about, changing our thinking to bring miracles into our lives. The principles are the same.

As we change thinking, we change consciousness; and as we change consciousness, we affect what happens in our world—and dominant thought prevails.

This means we need to focus our thinking on what we want and where we want to go with our lives. For example, why ever occupy your thinking with busy-body thoughts about other people and what they are doing or what they have done? This kind of thinking is empty and non-productive. Worse, if what you are thinking about other people is *negative*, you are impressing negative thoughts and negative patterns of thinking on *your* consciousness!

Your thinking needs to be consistent and correspond with your intention: Your miracle. Negative thinking *about anything* does not correspond with *anybody's* miracle. And, of course, when we have mixed thoughts about something, the resulting experience will correspond ultimately with our dominant belief.

You might compare your belief in any given area to a bird's nest. It is put together twig by twig, one at a time. While it may be unclear exactly what the nest will look like when it is finished, as each twig is put in place, the overall pattern becomes more apparent. Once it is finished, it will withstand great stress or efforts to unseat it; it is not easily changed; and, it takes a very strong wind to dislodge it. The same might well be said for the individual's consciousness.

It is important to understand that although we may want to change some of our current beliefs, we do not disrespect them. Remember that we developed them slowly, one thought at a time, over a long period of time. As they were formed, they represented the very best of our knowledge and ability at that time, so as we change them, we need to do so thoughtfully and respectfully.

There is no need or reason for any of us to punish ourselves for beliefs that may no longer serve us well. What we want to do is to take responsibility without taking or placing blame, to commend ourselves for making positive changes and to not criticize ourselves for doing the best we knew at the time.

THE THREE KEYS

Three keys that are already in your possession will open the door and make the magic begin. They are:

- Intention
- Decision
- Commitment

Intention sets the stage. Decision gets it started. And commitment makes it happen. Be open to your intention. It is the first signal that you are ready to make changes. The second key, decision, is a conscious choice, and you get to choose the time when you make your decision. Commitment is your conscious and continuous dedication to your decision.

So, in order to act on your intention to bring miracles into your life, *decide that you are going to think differently.* The third key in the miracle-making process—commitment—then provides the consistent effort needed to change old patterns of thinking and establish a new way of thinking. The change from "habitual thought" to what we call "trained thought"—the thought that makes miracles—takes conscious effort. We've all heard the adage, "Old habits die hard." This is especially true in changing our thought patterns. It requires a lot of consistent effort, and we do that with *commitment*—commitment to a better way of life—commitment to a more joyous life—commitment to changing our thinking—commitment to a miracle!

Can we think this way 100% of the time? I don't think so. But I doubt that the people using cognitive therapy do it 100% of the time either, and look at the wonderful strides they make! Once you change the overall focus of your thought patterns, just like with any other good habit, the power of that change carries over into other thought patterns as well.

Yet although we are responsible for creating the mental conditions that allow our miracle to manifest, we should never use force or manipulation to bring the miracle into our world. Nor should we block the miracle as it begins to take form, nor hinder its formation with negative thinking. *Allow* it to take form in its own way, and support it with positive thoughts.

**Let the miracle come through—
do not force, do not hinder.**

How do we do this?

THE POWER OF OUR WILL

All our lives, most of us have learned to try to make our circumstances better by changing them through the use of willpower, through a determined and willful effort to get, do and have the things we want.

Now, however, instead of trying to "make" things happen, you can learn to use your will to:

- Change your thinking.
- Control negative thinking and thought patterns.
- Release negative beliefs about yourself.
- Release negative beliefs about what you deserve in life.
- Shift your thinking in all these areas from negative to positive.
- Allow miracles to unfold in your life.

Is this a big job? It is... only if you *think* it is! You'll still have the same number of thoughts that you did before—only now they can be positive and life-enhancing. Remember the gold coins and lead coins. Take changes one day at a time, and congratulate yourself because you are now in the process of shifting your life from wherever it is now to something infinitely fuller, richer and more rewarding.

The best use of your will is a calm and peaceful determination to take control of your thinking at all times and to maintain a positive and focused mental acceptance of the good you desire no matter what happens.

Imagine a river moving toward the ocean. It goes over rocks, around bends and twigs, and sometimes down waterfalls, but it's always moving forward toward its goal—the ocean. You want to do the same thing as you move forward toward your goal, your good—your miracle. Remember:

- We are not creators; we are co-creators. We do not supply the power; we supply the direction.
- It is the Love, Power and Intelligence of Spirit responding to our thought that brings forth miracles.
- We control our thought by means of our will.

BLOW APART THE NEGATIVE, EXPAND THE POSITIVE

In order to have the miracles that we want in our lives, we need to take control of our thinking. Some people might say this is not possible—they believe that the way they think is the result of the circumstances in their lives *when, in fact, the circumstances in their lives are, in large part, due to the way they think.*

We *can* take control of our thinking. To do so, we need to make the decision and then commit to using our will to shift our thinking from negative to positive.

Although all thought is creative, not all thought has equal creative power. There is a big difference between the three various types of thought patterns that most of us use. These are:

- Random thoughts
- Habitual thought
- Trained thought

Random thoughts are those thoughts that flit through your mind uninvited and are gone before you know it. You always have a choice to entertain and expand on a random thought—or let it go right on through and out of your mind.

Especially if the random thought is *negative*, just let it go. To do this, some people visualize a "Stop" sign; others like to say to themselves something like, "Cancel! Cancel!" when they catch themselves with a negative thought.

Another really good idea came from a 15-year-old boy: He visualizes himself throwing a brick at the thought and watching as his negative thought or statement blows apart.

Use whatever works best for you. Just nip this kind of thinking in the bud, and make sure your subjective mind gets the right message and not the wrong one. If the thought is *positive*, you may want to allow it to expand. Let your train of thought stay in this positive mode of thinking and short-circuit or *"Cancel!"* any negative interruptions. Let this become an integral manner of thinking.

How we handle our random thoughts determines whether or not they become creative in our consciousness.

Habitual thought comprises the various thought patterns we have developed over our lifetimes: The way we look at things, at ourselves and at other people. Habitual thought is difficult to change because it "feels right" and is well-established. We've spent a lot of time developing and shaping the related beliefs in our consciousness, and everything in our consciousness is geared toward supporting them. For example, it was habitual thought that guided the reactions of people following September 11, 2001.

Just like any other habit, habitual thought works for us when it's positive and works against us when it's negative. So when we recognize negative habitual thinking, it's important to go to work and change it.

A very common form of negative habitual thinking is what I call "squirrel-caging." This is when we go over the same thing in our minds repeatedly—again and again— around, and around, and around. But, just like a squirrel running in a paddle-wheel-type cage, we're not *going* anywhere; we're not changing anything. All we're doing is filling our minds with negative thoughts and emotions.

The three primary areas where people tend to "squirrel-cage" are:

- When we feel we were "wronged" or insulted.
- When we make a mistake or otherwise embarrass ourselves.
- When we take a strong dislike to someone (this can be someone in our "inner circle" or someone we don't even know) and begin mentally criticizing everything they do.

Every time we start "squirrel-caging," we are recreating and reinforcing the associated negative emotion— usually, shame, embarrassment, anger, resentment or guilt. Sometimes we get caught up in these feelings and can't seem to break the cycle. It's almost like we're bound up in baling wire and can't get free.

We need to understand, first of all, that whenever we begin "squirrel-caging," all we are doing is filling our minds and bodies with negative thoughts, feelings and emotions. It's not solving anything in our lives, but it is leading to a lot of unresolved feelings. If there's something we can do, we need to do it (whether it's an apology, a discussion, etc.). Action can be very empowering. But, if there's nothing we can do or choose to do, then consider the following:

- See it as a learning experience.
- Recognize that it happened, it's over and it's okay.
- Realize it's in the past, and we can choose to not let it affect our life.
- Accept that it's time to let it go.
- Change it; leave it; accept it; or forget about it.

All this should be done sooner, rather than later.

Here is a very simple, directive statement that has worked wonders for many people when they realize they are in the throes of squirrel-caging:

"I don't need that any more!"

This statement has a tendency to "cut the baling wire" and allow the "squirrel-caging" to stop and normal thinking to resume. Any time the "squirrel caging" begins again, simply repeat to yourself, "I don't need that any more," and go on about your other business. Continue to do this, and your thought patterns will begin to move from negative to positive. Keep doing this as often as necessary.

Negative habitual thoughts are powerful habits developed over a period of years (how old are you?). Thankfully, it won't take nearly as long to change them as it did to form them. It may well take some effort, but it won't take any more time than if you don't change your thinking. And you'll end up in a much better place emotionally.

Trained thought intentionally and consistently focuses on what we want and not on what we don't want. It is focused; it is intentional; it is habitual; it is positive; and it lets the miracle come through.

**We develop trained thought
when we take charge of our thinking.**

Trained thought connects with and lets the Universal Power and Intelligence move in and through our lives in life-enhancing ways. As we nourish ourselves with life-enhancing trained thoughts, we gradually eliminate negatives that may have formed in our subjective mind.

Trained thought lets us express healthy living, abundant living, wonderful relationships and overall success in our lives. It brings good into our own lives, and also into the lives of others. It also brings about miracles!

Yet trained thought does not happen by chance—it is developed. And:

Trained thought is more powerful than untrained thought.

This is because it is *intentional, positive, focused and consistent*—a winning combination.

MAKE WAY FOR THE MIRACLE

There are three important steps to developing trained thought. Here's where your commitment and willpower support you.

(1) Begin to monitor your thoughts and speech in order to weed out negative thinking, including those thoughts or words that you might not think of as negative or as having much effect on your life. (A listing of these follows in the section on Habitual Negative Thinking that starts on page 107.)

(2) Consciously develop positive thought patterns about everything in your life (yourself, your world, your future, your family and friends—and especially your miracle).

(3) Unearth and transform the type of negative thinking (e.g., guilt, worry, envy, resentment, fear, the

past, etc.) that blocks the flow of good in your world

When you begin to monitor your thoughts, you may find that there are a lot of negative thoughts, feelings and emotions that we direct toward ourselves and others. But, because they don't always *appear* to carry a strong emotional charge, we are often unaware of them. Or we think they're harmless.

Well, they're *not* harmless. They often comprise a steady stream of judgmental negatives throughout the day. Be aware of their negative consequences:

- Negative thoughts divert thought power from our miracle. We can only think one thing at a time, so every time we think negatively we can never recapture that opportunity for a positive thought.

- Negative thoughts tend to set us up for negative situations without our ever knowing it. One negative thought by itself doesn't seem like much. But remember, all too often, most of our thinking is repetitive. One little negative thought which repeats itself again and again sets up fields of negative energy which begin to attract negative experiences.

- Negative thoughts attract more of the same into our world. Notice that when you begin thinking about something, your thought moves pretty consistently in one direction or another. For example, when you're thinking positively, you go from one positive thought to another and then another, energizing yourself and everything you're creating in your world. When you think negatively, you attract more negative thoughts—and those, in turn, create their own emotional energy. Soon you're deep into some strong negative thinking—worrying about all the things that might go wrong, rehearsing what you'll do and say, remembering all the times in your life things didn't work out, and so on. Someone I know once observed, "Negative thoughts are like wire coat hangers. You let one in, and pretty soon you have a closet full."

Here's a simple axiom that will help you remember why it's so important to shift your thought from negative to positive:

**Power flows toward and magnifies
that to which you give your attention.**

All thought is creative—negative as well as positive. The Creative Force of Spirit is always responding, and does not judge or question the demands we place on it through our dominant thought patterns. Thus it moves to bring either negative or positive experiences into our lives.

So when our thinking and attention are focused in positive, life-enhancing channels, the Intelligence and Power of Spirit moves into our world in positive, life-enhancing directions. This gradually modifies our core beliefs from negative, limiting beliefs to positive, miracle-making beliefs and expectations.

HABITUAL NEGATIVE THINKING

As discussed earlier, "squirrel-caging" is a repetitive way of thinking about something. There are many "somethings" that we think about, and—without even trying—we can find ourselves "squirrel-caging" about them.

Here are six common areas of negative thinking. They represent some habitual ways of reacting to our experiences. All of them have an enormous impact in blocking our miracles because we often add a lot of emotional power to these areas of thinking.

Ask yourself which of these are most familiar in your own thinking. Almost all of us express all of these patterns at one time or another. If you do not recognize all of them as being negative, think about the axiom, "Power flows toward and magnifies that to which you give your attention," and then take time to be clear on just why they are usually counter-productive thought patterns.

Again, remember that it takes many years to form these patterns of thinking, so if you recognize any of them in yourself, it's important to be gentle and patient with yourself. Rather than punishing yourself, commit to shifting yourself gradually into better thought patterns.

1. Complaining—When we complain, in some subtle way we are saying that the problem needs to be "fixed" by someone other than ourselves. And this, of course, implies that we can't do anything about it. Yes, complaining really reflects a sense of powerlessness. We complain and complain, hoping that somewhere, somehow, our plaintive cries will activate someone else to solve the unpleasant or unfair situation in which we find ourselves. Instead of empty griping and complaining, aim for a well-thought-out and relatively unemotional effort to correct a problem.

> **Concentrate on the solution,
> not on the problem.
> Change it, leave it, accept it
> or forget about it!**

2. Blaming—Whenever we blame, we are telling the Universe that someone else is responsible for the problem. By doing this, we place our power "over there" rather than "right here." This whole book is intended to illustrate the power we have in creating our world. But we first must recognize and claim that power. Don't give your power away by blaming!

> **Take responsibility for your own life.
> You are not a victim other than by choice.**

3. Self-criticism (in any form)—This goes to the very core of our beliefs.

The way we treat ourselves in our habitual thinking is a reflection of our current self-image. Since the Universal Creative Power takes us at our word, if we want life to treat us well, we need to start by thinking positively about ourselves.

This can be a big job for many of us, but we can start by making a written list of our qualities and our positive attributes. It is especially important to not criticize ourselves for past behavior. Every time we put ourselves down, we are limiting the positive flow of good into our world. We need to know that our good comes from a Universal Creative Force that is always ready to provide for us in positive ways. We can be open to it, or we can close it off. When we criticize ourselves, we are telling the Universe that we don't really deserve good things in our lives. Remember, the one who says, "I can," and the one who says, "I can't," are both right.

Become your own biggest booster—all the time!

4. Criticism (including, but not limited to, gossip)— This usually seems so innocuous that it's hard to imagine it could have a negative impact on our own lives, but whenever we are bad-mouthing another or judging someone else negatively, we are establishing an overall "field" of discord or disharmony in our consciousness. When we look around and see only things we don't like, the Creative Force of the Universe responds and provides more things for us not to like. Remember we have an entire Universe responding to us, taking us at our word, so:

- Look for things you like about your experiences.
- Look for things you admire about people.
- Make sure your suggestions are constructive and loving.

5. The "Could'a, Should'a, Would'a" Syndrome— This syndrome is common in many people who beat themselves up over something that happened in the past. Another expression of this syndrome is to look back and say, "If only this," or "If only that." Guilt and regret are subtle attempts to change the past. We can't redo the past—but we can change the way we look at it, and we can learn from it. Once we have reviewed a past situation, taken the good from it and learned its lessons, we need to let it go, so:

- Stop hitting yourself over the head.
- You can't "should'a done" anything.
- Review your good qualities, and move on!

6. Envy—When we envy someone for what they have, we are subtly telling ourselves that not only don't we have that, but even more importantly, we probably won't ever have it. Consider this example of two people both looking at the same beautiful home. The first one thinks, "Ah, that's gorgeous! One day I will own a home at least as beautiful as that." The second one thinks, "Oh, wow! Look at that beautiful home. It almost makes me ache inside to see it. I'd love something like that, but I know it won't happen." The first person is mentally accepting (or "claiming") an equivalent home for themselves, while the second is mentally separating themselves from it because they don't believe it's possible for them. Both are probably right. (By the way, "wish" is in the same category as "hope" and "try"—non-attainment is implicit in the word itself.)

When we envy someone for what they are, we are actually putting ourselves down big time! We may not realize it, but we already do have the same quality as that other person (or an equivalent quality of our own). All of us are created with an innate birthright to express the great and wonderful gifts of Life in ways that are unique and individual to each of us. But we first need to believe it so that our special gifts are not blocked but expressed into the world.

> Learn to admire people for what they have and what they have accomplished. Know that you, too, can accomplish wonderful things—things consistent with your own unique essence and desires. The Infinite provides an endless supply of good.

Commitment is one thing; *consistent commitment* is another. At first, thinking in a new way may seem like a lot of effort but it gets progressively easier as we begin re-forming our thought patterns. An important axiom to remember here is:

Nature abhors a vacuum.

This means that when we are monitoring our thinking, we cannot simply "erase" a negative thought. If we do, it will simply pop right back a second later—and it will keep popping back longer than we can possibly keep erasing it because our old habitual thought will be at work. What we need to do is to:

Replace the negative thought with positive thought.

For example, it's easy to be judgmental about people—even people we don't know, or barely know. Whenever this happens to you, try this: Observe rather than react. See if you can find something about the person to really appreciate. Or, see them with warmth and compassion rather than with criticism. Remember the old saying about not judging someone else until we've walked a mile in their shoes. Remind yourself that this would be a pretty dull world if we were all alike. Enjoy the variety of life.

No, this is not Pollyanna-ish. Thought is a precious commodity. Why would you consciously choose to use it to criticize someone else when you can use it to make your own life better? Why choose lead coins rather than gold? If what the other person is doing has no real impact on your life, why give them "free rent" in your mind? Why identify yourself with negative conduct? Your conscious mind may be judging, but your subjective mind is not. Your subjective mind is simply *accepting* the focus of your attention and producing negative experiences in your world!

Now, let's assume for a moment that the person you're being judgmental about did something that really *does* seem to affect your world. If there is something you can do to correct it, then do it, and then let it go. By dwelling on it and giving it emotional power in your mind, you are, in effect, telling your subjective mind that this person has the power to hurt you in some way—or that they *have* hurt you or *might* hurt you. If that's what you believe, you won't be wrong. On the other hand, you can choose to affirm:

> "There is endless and abundant good in this universe and in my world. No one and no thing can hurt me or harm me or take my good from me. There is a Creative Intelligence in me that knows exactly how to correct this situation."

GETTING STARTED

Now, let's get a handle on exactly what negatives there may be in your thinking that need to be released and replaced.

Here are three exercises that will help you identify your negative thoughts. All of them will give you a really good start toward developing a consciousness of trained thought.

Get a small spiral notebook and carry it with you everywhere for a period of two days. Every time a negative thought comes into your mind, make a little mark on the notebook. Count the marks by 5's so you can get an idea of how frequently these thoughts come into your mind each day. Then break them down by mornings, afternoons and evenings to see if you're more positive at certain times of the day.

If you can't manage to do this for two days because it's simply too much, then do it for two hours a day. But get started with it, because in order to change your thinking you first have to know what it is in your thinking that needs changing.

In addition to giving you an idea of your frequency of negative thinking, this exercise will also give you an idea of the types of negative thoughts you entertain if you make note of them.

When you have identified the types of negative thoughts currently running through your mind, choose positive thoughts to replace them. And, from that time on, whenever one of the negative thoughts pops up, your job is to replace it with something positive.

You may be astonished at the results when you first do this exercise. Most people find that until they actually keep track, it's almost impossible to grasp the frequency and type of negative thinking they entertain.

The next two exercises are Buddhist exercises. They are taken from an ancient teaching called "Quam" (which is "contacting Spirit with conscious awareness"). I am grateful to my friend, Tian of Siam, a former Miss Thailand, for sharing them. She is a beautiful person with a beautiful consciousness.

The first one is called "Conscientious Continuity." Do it every day for thirty days. It's such great training that you may want to make it permanent!

Sit quietly at a time in which you know you will not be interrupted. For a period of ten minutes, allow only positive thoughts to remain in your mind. Entertain only a positive stream-of-consciousness. Simply dismiss and release any negative thoughts as you hold fast to your true self.[3]

If you have difficulty with staying focused like this for ten minutes, begin with five, or even three, and build up to ten. This exercise is centering, and very rewarding.

The next exercise is good to do occasionally (maybe once a week at first). As we have discussed, complaining is negative—but often we feel compelled to explain, justify or rationalize our complaining. Well, that's negative, too! This exercise does two things. First, it helps form a pattern of not complaining, and second, it blocks any habit we may have of explaining or making excuses for our negativity (e.g., "After all, who wouldn't feel this way?").

> For an entire twenty-four hours, try not to complain or speak negatively about anyone. Also, try not to explain or make excuses for any negative statements or complaining.[4]

Yes, I used the word "try." When you do the exercise, you will know why. Most people find this exercise a real challenge even when they have learned to direct their thinking into positive channels. (Does this tell you something about the amount of negative thinking most of us entertain?)

I encourage you not to skip these three exercises. They will definitely make you aware of what some might think of as "little" or "unimportant" negatives in their thinking. They'll also make you aware of the more powerful negative thinking patterns that you may have developed.

On the upside, however, the last two exercises will definitely help make you feel more centered and "connected" to Spirit.

IT'S EASY TO RATIONALIZE

As we begin intentionally selecting only gold coins for our consciousness, it becomes a step-by-step process. Most of our negative thinking is an automatic response to conditions or circumstances that relate to a core belief—and, as we discussed, we have been reinforcing such beliefs for years. Because our responses are so automatic, our minds often play games with us so we won't want to do the necessary work. We can rationalize our way out of mental exercise just as easily as we can out of physical exercise. It's as though the old thought patterns have lots of "mental soldiers" to defend them and keep them in place!

Be gentle and supportive with yourself—much of our self-talk is self-deprecating and that's part of what we want to change. It's especially helpful to remember "Cancel! Cancel!" or "I don't need this anymore" whenever you start beating up on yourself. We can all work more at being our own best friend rather than our biggest critic. All of us can use more gold coins in our thinking about ourselves.

If the process seems daunting, keep in mind that this is not an "all-or-nothing" program. It's a process, and you won't do it all at once. It took years to develop your current patterns of thought. From now on:

- Congratulate yourself every time you catch and correct any negative thinking or any one of the more powerful habitual thought patterns.

- See each one as an immediate step toward your miracle and as a big step toward a life filled with miracles.
- Look forward, not backwards.
- Remind yourself that "yesterday ended last night" and you are now moving step by step down a new and wonderful path on your life journey.
- Rich and unexpected rewards begin to manifest in your life as you move along your new path.

A TOWER OF POWER

Almost all of us have some combination of both positive and negative core beliefs about ourselves. Sometimes, especially during a time of crisis, we may find a strong, hidden belief that is ready to flower—a "tower of power," so to speak. Sheldon was a person who had such a belief.

He was a particularly kind and gentle man, a jeweler in Chicago whom I had known for years. He was probably in his early seventies when, one spring day, he told me he had been diagnosed with prostate cancer. This was in 1980, and the only known medical treatment at that time was surgery. So, Sheldon was scheduled for surgery the following week at the Mayo Clinic in Rochester, Minnesota. He was frightened. He didn't want the surgery. And he didn't want to die.

We met for lunch, and we talked for a very long time about miracle-making principles and about the power of belief and expectancy. Sheldon said that everything I was saying resonated with him at a deep level.

As we spoke, he felt a great calm and a greater certainty that an "Inner Intelligence" in him knew exactly what to do to heal his physical body. He also said that it felt as though he had known these "Truths" for his entire life but had never been able to articulate them. We also talked about how he could use his willpower to "control his thought" and how he could transform his thinking into positive channels.

Together, we decided on some affirmations for him to say and read to himself, and I gave him a copy of my booklet, *Something Good is About to Happen*, about the power of positive expectancy.

The following week, Sheldon called to tell me he had decided to cancel his scheduled surgery. Sheldon's wife, who did not understand or agree with what he was doing, was frightened and upset. They had several lengthy conversations, and although she still didn't understand or approve, she did agree to keep her fears and concerns to herself.

Sheldon refused to entertain any negative conversation or comments from anyone. His resolve was very strong and he was adamant about no negativity.

During the following weeks, Sheldon and I met again several times to talk about his wholeness. Seldom have I known anyone to evidence the total faith Sheldon had in healing through the power of the mind.

We prayed together, and he continued with his daily affirmations and meditations.

That Thanksgiving, I received a letter from Sheldon—giving great thanks that he was alive and totally free of any trace of cancer ANYWHERE! Sheldon lived another fourteen healthy, productive years, active in all ways.

Not everybody has the innate belief, ready and waiting to express itself, that Sheldon had, nor should everyone cancel surgery. For many people, the shortcut is a little different. But the beauty of the path I'm pointing you toward is that it leads not to experiencing just one miracle but to the development of a "miracle-making consciousness."

A few years ago, I was working with another man to help him learn these principles. After a while, he said, "You know, this is really discouraging. I feel like a kid again back in school with all the 'should's' and 'shouldn'ts'."

Think for a moment about the attitude that his comment reflected: That it was too emotionally heavy a burden for him. It's just as easy to say to yourself, "Isn't this terrific! I can change all this negative thinking that weighs me down emotionally—and at the same time, I will change my life. I'm learning how to make miracles!"

Think of the process not as any form of limitation, but rather as having a wonderful choice in your thinking—a choice that allows you to change your world.

Each one of us has exactly the same twenty-four hours a day in which to think. Each of us chooses what we will think about; each of us gets to choose any combination of gold coins or lead coins.

Where you go from here is up to you. You can use the next few days, weeks and months (yes, even years) thinking what you always thought and getting what you always got, or you can change your world. You can make miracles! The choice is yours.

The real shortcut is in finally knowing what to do and doing it. Now you know! Don't waste your time or limit your life any longer! Make some miracles!

PART THREE

MAKING MIRACLES

There are two ways you can live your life; as if NOTHING is a miracle; or as if EVERYTHING is a miracle.

— ALBERT EINSTEIN —

CHAPTER 6

HOW TO MAKE MIRACLES

HE was thirty-two years old as he stood on the shores of Lake Michigan fully intending to throw himself into the lake to commit suicide. Five years earlier, his oldest child had died at the age of four. The intervening years had been long and painful. On that gut-wrenching day, he was virtually penniless. He was disgraced. He had failed miserably in his business efforts, and many people he cared about had lost money because of him. And now, there was a new baby but there was no money to feed her—or his wife—or himself. If he got himself out of the way, he thought, at least his wife and baby would be taken care of by his family.

He stood there a long time—a very long time—thinking. He looked at the rocks and the pebbles. He watched the waves. As he did this, his mind began to calm and his thinking began to clear. Then, he had a realization, a higher awareness, an inner knowing. It was as though a voice said to him, "You do not belong to yourself. You belong to the universe." As he followed this realization further, he recognized that the voice came from within him and from nowhere else. This led him to make a new commitment: *To always endeavor to think for himself.* No longer would he be influenced or swayed by the opinions or theories of others.

His next question to himself concerned a universal philosophical question. As he had done many times in the past, he explored the possibility of a greater intellect operating in the universe. This time, however, he found his answer was swift and positive. He could look back on his own life experience and recognize that the things that happened to him were not random occurrences. He saw in his life the orderliness of interactive principles that operated without exception. He was profoundly moved by what he recognized as spiritual insights, so much so that he made a sacred commitment to himself and this greater Power to spend the rest of his life solving problems that affect everyone on the planet.

The man's name was Buckminster Fuller. Fortunately for all of us, he lived for another fifty-six years, during which time he became recognized as an inventor, architect, engineer, mathematician, poet and cosmologist.

Among his accomplishments, he received twenty-five U.S. patents and wrote twenty-eight books. He was awarded honorary doctorates from forty-seven colleges and universities and received dozens of major architectural and design awards, including Gold Medal awards from both the American Institute of Architects and the Royal Institute of British Architects. He was a tireless world traveler whose lectures are still remembered by those fortunate to have heard him.

Fuller is remembered as one of the most remarkable and visionary men of the twentieth century. Albert Einstein once said to him with great respect, "Young man, you amaze me!"

Buckminster Fuller is probably best known today for his invention of what is called the "geodesic dome. " This is the lightest, strongest and most cost-effective structure ever devised. Incredibly, the larger the dome, the more proportionally stronger and lighter it becomes. There is still another amazing aspect of this incredible invention— Buckminster Fuller *actually saw the basic structure of the geodesic dome in the pebbles on the shores of Lake Michigan as he stood there pondering suicide.*

Years later, this same basic structure would also provide the basic structure of space platforms which, as of this writing, are on the drawing board for future construction by NASA.[1]

So what happened that fateful day? How did this penniless young man, a failure, a person hopeless and destitute, turn his life around to become one of the luminaries of the twentieth century?

He saw himself as a channel of life through which the Universal Creative Force finds expression.

Buckminster Fuller didn't make the miracles that took place in his life after that day on the shores of Lake Michigan. No, what he did was to let go of the feeling of being a hapless victim. What he did was to follow his own intuitive guidance and the emotional drive that began to spontaneously generate within him.

What he did was to open to the Power and Intelligence that does make miracles.

In every one of the cases we've talked about, including Buckminster Fuller's, the people involved didn't stop "doing" but they did stop struggling. They did not see themselves as victims. Instead, they had faith in and opened to a Higher Power (call it whatever you choose).

They focused their thinking on the positive outcome rather than mentally fearing and fighting the negative.

The difference may seem subtle, but it's a difference that turns lives around.

Does this seem like something you can do? Of course you can! It's *your* mind, and they're *your* thoughts, and *you* have control over them. Does this mean you'd better not ever have a negative thought or a bad idea? No, not at all. Frankly, I doubt that any of us will ever come to that point—or at least I don't know anyone who has. What it does mean is that you must consistently monitor your thinking and gently but firmly release negative thoughts and replace them with positive ones.

By doing this, we also do the following:

We change our thinking—in order to...
Change our consciousness—in order to...
Change our lives.

Before going further, let's review the five factors that form the foundation for a miracle-making attitude. These factors are probably more meaningful and understandable to you now than when we discussed them in Chapter 2. Read them carefully. Be sure you understand each one of them.

- Miracles unfold according to Universal Law.
- Your miracle is possible.
- Your miracle is never too big.
- You play a major role.
- You deserve miracles in your life.

If you have difficulty accepting any of the five, stop right now and take the time to understand what it is that's blocking your acceptance. If necessary, go back to Chapter 2 and review them. Developing a sound, miracle-making attitude is important.

Your miracle-making attitude is actually the beginning of the miracle itself.

Miracles just don't seem to happen to people who don't believe in them. Moreover, when they do happen to people who don't think they deserve the good that has come into their lives, that good usually doesn't seem to last. This is the Law of Belief in action (page 69).

Remember that when we talk about your "good," of course, we are talking about whatever it is that you desire in your life. It's up to you to define it. You get to choose what "good" looks like in your experience.

There is no limit to the type of good or variety of areas in which you are able to experience your good, nor is there any limit to the amount of good available to you in any given area. The Power and Intelligence expressing through you is inexhaustible. So is the good it can bring into our lives.

MAKING A MIRACLE—ANY MIRACLE

Essentially, there are four major areas in our lives where we feel we need or want a miracle. These are health, abundance (prosperity), relationships and success (creative expression.) Although there are some specific areas of focus and attention for each of these, there are very important parts of the process that are the same for *any* miracle in *any* area of your life. So, let's talk about those.

1. Be very clear.

You need to be very clear about the miracle you desire— about the good you want in your world. You can't be fuzzy and you can't be indecisive. You are the only thinker in your world, and the only communication you have with the Power and Intelligence that makes your miracle happen is through your thinking, through your consciousness. So, don't equivocate on what it is you want—really want.

As you do this, however, it is important to focus also on what might be called the "qualities of good" that this miracle will bring into your life. For example—

- If it is a new job, think about how good you will feel coming home after spending a busy but rewarding day in this new position where your talents are allowed to express and benefit yourself and others.

- If your miracle is a return to good health, get the feeling of how good it will feel to be doing all the things you enjoy and doing them with ease.

- If your miracle is a wonderful new relationship, don't focus only on the qualities you desire in this person. See yourself enjoying leisure time together, and allow yourself to feel the warmth and loving comfort of this togetherness.

When you do this, you are making your miracle very real. This not only assists in clarifying what it is that you want, but it does two other things as well. First, it "puts you in the picture." If it's your miracle, you need to be an integral part of it—living it, tasting it, enjoying it and being one with it. Second, as you "put yourself in the picture," you respond emotionally, almost as though you were living the experience. Emotion is the fire that intensifies your desire and really gets things moving on the invisible plane. Adding the emotional feeling of *completion* is very powerful.

As you clearly visualize or imagine your miracle, it's important to focus *only on the end result* of what you want, and not the means by which it comes about. In other words:

Focus on the "what," not the "how" or the "when."

Let the "how" be up to this Infinite Intelligence that's working for you in response to your thinking.

For example, I have a friend named Martha who had always wanted to tour Europe, but her time was limited and so were her finances. After she attended a visualization class where she learned to spend some time each day focused on the visualization of things she wanted to experience as a reality in her world, she began to focus on a European trip. She saw herself walking the streets of Rome. She saw herself shopping in London.

She did not focus on "how" and she did not focus on "when."

Shortly before Christmas, she ran into a friend she hadn't seen in a long time. When the friend asked her the customary, "What's new?" Martha was astonished to hear herself respond, "I'm going to Europe." No, she confessed to her friend, she didn't know just when and she didn't know just where, but she knew she was going. She was even more astonished when her friend said to her, "I have three vouchers for European travel, and I can't use them. I'll send them to you as soon as I get home." Martha is a teacher, and between the time she ran into her friend and the time that school resumed after the holidays, she had the trip of her life traveling to Rome, Amsterdam, London and Athens—all for free!

> Make sure it's what you want, not what somebody else wants—or, worse yet, what you think somebody else wants for you.

The authentic part of us is the only part that can express freely, joyously and whole-heartedly. There is always resistance when we are trying to live someone else's dream or fulfill someone else's desire for us. To live his own life and follow his own inner guide was one of the insights that Buckminster Fuller had.

> Is the miracle you desire so clear in your mind that you can write it down in one clear sentence? Then do so. Do so now.

And as soon as you can, get a journal and write it down again. Call it your "Miracle Journal" if you wish. If your desire is not yet that clear, then take the time to set it down in one unequivocal sentence. Clarify it in your mind because this establishes the focus of your attention.

2. Expect the best.

Here comes the Law of Expectancy, remember? (page 76.) We need to consciously invoke this Law by expecting the best, even when negative circumstances appear—in fact, especially when negative circumstances appear. Remember that we tend to attract that which we love, fear or steadily expect.

All too often, we expect far less than we really want. The reason for that is that we don't think we can have what we really want.

When we expect *less* than what we want, we get *less* than what we want.

Remind yourself, if necessary, that you *do* deserve the good you desire. You deserve it by the right of your very existence. Let go of any and all old messages to the contrary. Reaffirm, as often as necessary, that you deserve your miracle. You deserve the best. This is extremely important, because this changes your consciousness from a lower expectancy to a greater and progressively greater expectancy. The Creative Principle is always responding to you at the level of your belief and acceptance.

- Our purpose is not to create—
- Our purpose is to co-create—
- And to do that, we let loose the creative action of Spirit.

We don't have to beg the Law to work any more than we have to beg electricity to work when we turn on a lamp. It's a principle, remember? It always works, and it always works the same way.

We need to consciously and consistently expect that everything is working for our greatest and highest good. We need to trust. More than that, we need to have faith in the perfect operation of the Power and Intelligence working for and through us.

We are working with a creative Law that works by Itself and that responds to our thinking—our negative thinking as well as our positive thinking. If you're afraid you'll never get it, guess what! You won't! You'll never get it if you don't first accept it for yourself.

Your responsibility is to get to a feeling of real acceptance of the good you desire, a feeling of completion. The responsibility of Spirit is to get us from where we are to where we want to be.

You do not have to settle for second best.

It is your spiritual inheritance, your very birthright, to have health, prosperity, success and good relationships expressing in life-enhancing ways. No, you do not have to settle for second best.

3. Let go of fear.

It really doesn't matter whether it's fear about our (or someone else's) health, finances or loss of a relationship. Fear is faith in something negative. It would seem that if we are clear about the good that we want, and we are expecting the best, there would be no room left for fear, right? Well, not exactly. In the back of our minds, we tend to hold onto many reasons why we might not get what we desire. Don't let this fear control you!

Don't back off from what you want because you're afraid you might not get it.

This can be a real challenge, particularly if you are facing a life-threatening illness, the loss of a job, the end of a marriage or the loss of any important relationship. I didn't originate the following statement, but I've used it for so many years that I can't remember where it came from.

Fear is faith turned inside out.

Think of faith and fear as being opposite ends of the same continuum. The more afraid we are of the future, the more fearful we become.

The greater our expectancy of good, however, the stronger our faith. And the stronger our faith, the greater our expectancy of good.

This is not blind faith. I'm not talking about wishful thinking that hopes that some whimsical Higher Power just might give us what we want. I'm talking about a Creative Action that is inexhaustible and perpetual.

In making our miracles, we are actually directing Universal Power and Intelligence, and we want to do it in full confidence that It will respond. In a very real sense, we are directing the universe! We are—each of us—the key player in allowing our miracle(s) to unfold.

Remember: We magnify and increase that to which we give our attention. The Love, Power and Intelligence of the Universe is always ready and waiting to do Its part whenever *we* provide the channel for It to do so. Think of it this way:

> Through our oneness with Spirit,
> our highest hopes and worst fears
> become definite possibilities.
> Which it is to be is up to us.
> The choice is ours.
> Whichever we think about most,
> that's where the Power goes.

Some years ago, I was going through a very frightening experience in my life, and I found myself simply unable to feel the faith that I wanted. Not only was I fearful, but since I understand the power of negative thoughts, feelings and emotions, I even began to worry about my fearful feelings. This went on until one morning, during a period of quiet contemplation, I finally allowed myself to address this—to recognize it and stop pushing the fear aside by denying it. As I did this, I had a wonderful realization that *I didn't have to have 100% faith in order for my problem to begin turning around.*

All we need is 51% faith and our lives begin to turn in the right direction.

With this recognition, I was able to relax. My faith was actually far stronger than my fear, and as I realized this, I began to feel very empowered, and my faith became more and more self-generating.

President Franklin D. Roosevelt led our nation from the deep depression of the 1930's to victory during World War II with these simple words, "The only thing we have to fear is fear itself." I wonder if he knew how spiritually powerful his words were and are.

Most times, the change in consciousness that we need for our miracle doesn't happen overnight.

Usually our change in consciousness is incremental, and day by day we feel a growing power and confidence.

This is why we need to be watchful about our thinking: Our thoughts magnetically attract others like themselves. For example, when we think negatively, our minds will go on a stream-of-consciousness journey into all sorts of related realms of negativity until we consciously stop ourselves. We start thinking of all the bad things that can happen or that we have heard of happening to someone else. We imagine future conversations in which we talk with others about how we are handling all these (imaginary) sad things in our lives. If we want miracles in our lives, this kind of thinking has to change.

Stop your negative thinking and replace it immediately with a positive flow of thoughts.

To do this, use the same stream-of-consciousness process, but in a positive way. We want the imaginary conversations to be about all the good things taking place in our lives. We want to let our minds take us to new heights of success. We want to *feel* the joy and happiness we expect to experience when our miracle has manifested. This is what Virginia was doing as she visualized the doctor telling her, "There is no aneurysm."

We want the expectancy of our miracle to be so complete that we feel as though the miracle already exists or is beginning to exist in our life. Touch it; feel it; taste it; live it.

4. Open your mind to all possibilities.

When we open to a greater flow of Universal Power and Intelligence in our world, we also need to let go of trying to control people and conditions to make the outcome exactly the way we want it. When we open to all possibilities, we are allowing this Creative Power to express in ways that are much greater than any we might have imagined. This does not mean abdicating our right to make choices and decisions, but it does mean letting go of trying to change our life by changing all the outer circumstances or by changing or manipulating other people.

Although miracles always unfold in a very natural manner, they often come through unexpected channels. Whenever we hold tight, mentally or physically, to having things unfold "our way," we run the risk of delaying our good, diminishing it or even blocking it altogether.

"What" is up to you. "How" is up to Spirit.

This is a new way of thinking for most people. Essentially it means not being locked in to only one solution. It means knowing that what looks like an obstacle may very well be a steppingstone to a better unfoldment of your miracle. For example, in Chapter 4 when Tom learned that the loan company's virtual commitment fell through, he remained grounded in his conviction that the success of his company was assured. He knew that whatever he needed was forthcoming, and it was. It simply came through a different channel.

This way of thinking also means having a calm mind. The more anxious, fragmented and negative our thinking, the less receptive we are to the guidance of the Infinite. In some ways, our minds are like a wireless radio. They transmit and they receive, but if there is a lot of static, their transmission and reception are affected. Negativity is damaging, for it can turn us away from the good that is actually knocking at our door.

5. See yourself as you want to be.

This ties in closely with "Expect the best," but sometimes we can expect the best but not put ourselves in the picture. Yet this is *the single most powerful thing we can do to set into motion the Law of Expectancy.*

To illustrate, we can expect to get well, but until we are able to "see ourselves healthy," we have not really created a mental image of health for ourselves.

- If we desire health, we need to see ourselves healthy and filled with energy and enthusiasm for life.

- If we desire abundance, we need to see ourselves enjoying an abundant lifestyle.

- If we want a healing in a relationship, we need to feel warm and loving vibrations for the other person or people and see the relationship as we would like it to be.

- If we want business success, we need to feel ourselves successful with the mental assurance that the success we desire is even right now unfolding in our lives.

Now, this doesn't mean that we disregard where we are and what we have to handle. When we talk about positive thoughts and emotions, we don't mean that we should ever live in a state of denial. We need to think at the level of Spirit (the "Above") as well as at the level of the world in which we live (the "Below"). In his book *It's All God*, Walter Starcke calls this "double-thinking" and that's exactly what it is.

We are clear about the facts of the situation, and we handle whatever has to be handled regarding the situation. But while we are doing all of this, our thinking about where we are headed is focused on what we *want*, not on what we don't want or where we are today.

6. Keep the power. Don't talk about it.

For many people, this is very difficult, but keeping the idea of your miracle secret is extremely important for several reasons. Can you think back to a time when you were very excited about something good that was going to happen in your life and you shared it prematurely with someone? Did you have a deflated or somewhat empty feeling right afterwards? If so, that's very common because some of the Power of your idea was dissipated in the sharing.

Further, a negative or envious person is bound to contribute a certain amount of negative energy, either spoken or unspoken, around your idea. They are likely to tell others and might even have a good laugh about it. Or, they might openly dismiss your wonderful idea in a way that negatively affects your own thinking about it.

The integrity of the relationship between you and Spirit with respect to the unfoldment of your miracle must not be violated.

Sometimes the Power of the idea of your miracle is so great, you think you will explode if you don't share it. When this happens, *keep this Power.* Don't ever share it just to share it. Wait until it is absolutely necessary for you to share your idea in order for it to continue unfolding. Even then, share as little as possible with as few people as possible.

7. Do what needs to be done *by you.*

Just as you are the only thinker in your world, you are also the one who makes the choices of what is to be done or not done. Yes, through the Law of Attraction, many good things move into our lives, apparently unbidden. But almost always, there are things that you need to do and choices you need to make. When you are very clear about what it is you want or need, your mind becomes calm and focused. This, in turn, provides a clear channel for the guidance and direction you need in making your choices and decisions about what to do—whether it's choosing the right doctor or taking the right job.

Spirit works for us by working through us.

There are things that only you can do, and you need to do them. And when you are clear in what you want, and you expect the best, and you are open to all possibilities, you can make your decisions with calmness and an assurance that your decisions are the right ones. Use the following affirmation:

As I make this decision, I know that the path of wrong action is sealed, and only the path of right action remains open.

This type of affirmation opens you to the flow of Universal Intelligence in guiding your decisions. It alleviates fear, and you can then make your decisions with complete confidence that everything is working for your greatest and highest good.

8. Pray. Pray often.

You may wonder why this wasn't item #1, and from one point of view, perhaps it should have been. However, from another point of view:

When—
- You are very clear in what you want, and
- You expect the best, and
- You have released fear, and
- You are open to all possibilities, and
- Your intentions are good, and

- You are prepared to do whatever needs to be done by you, then
- You have established a powerful mental foundation for your prayer.

Add to this foundation the emotional power of your joyous expectation of good, and you have established a power base stronger than any other.

Many of those who have developed a personal spiritual practice regularly spend time in meditation before they do their prayer work. Meditation is a wonderful gateway to prayer because it is a time of quiet solitude and of opening to the Infinite Power of the Universe. It is also a time which leads to great insights and answers. This powerful practice is discussed more fully in Chapter 11.

Prayer is effective whether we're praying for ourselves, praying for others, or being prayed for by others. Many scientific studies done over the past twenty or twenty-five years demonstrate conclusively that prayer has a positive effect, not only on continuing health and longevity, but also on the degree, as well as ease and speediness, of recovery following illness or surgery. Although these studies, of necessity, have been done in the area of physical healing, the principle is the same in all areas of our lives (health, prosperity, relationships and success).

Prayer works.

About eight years ago, I was a guest at a seminar given by Dr. Larry Dossey to a group of medical students, residents and interns at Chicago's Rush-Presbyterian St. Luke's Hospital. As Dossey addressed the power of prayer, one of the attendees asked, "Are you saying that in future years we might be considered guilty of malpractice if we do not pray for our patients?" Dossey replied, "Well, if you know something works and you don't use it… ." He smiled and left the sentence unfinished.

In recent years, there has been a dramatic increase in the medical community's recognition of the power of prayer. Less than a decade ago, only three of America's 125 medical schools offered courses on prayer and physical healing. Today, that number has increased to seventy-nine.[2]

People who pray regularly appear to live longer—as much as eight years longer, according to a study of over 6,000 Americans.[3] Working with MRI scans, Harvard researcher Herbert Benson, M.D. (author of *The Relaxation Response*) has shown that when we pray, we actually switch off "stress" pathways in the brain and activate pathways that promote healing and calm.[4]

Not only has prayer been shown to add to our longevity, it also affects the quality of our lives. Many of the studies that have been done in this regard are quite dramatic. For example, in a recent study, conducted by Roger A. Lobo, M.D., at Columbia University, a group of 199 women undergoing in vitro fertilization were randomly assigned to be prayed for by a group of strangers in the United States, Canada and Australia. Neither the women's doctors nor the women themselves were aware of this. The researchers expected that the results would show no benefit from prayer. They were astonished when the normally low success rate of in vitro fertilization (ranging from 22% to 26%) *jumped to 50% for these women.*[5]

Praying for another is called "intercessory prayer," and it's effective because, as we have so clearly established in earlier chapters, we are all interconnected—not only with each other but also with the Source of our being.

> Our prayers are effective for ourselves,
> for others and in all areas of our lives.

When we understand the Spiritual laws and the scientific discoveries we have already discussed (especially relative to the interconnectedness of all life), it is easy to see how and why prayer is effective in *all* areas of our lives. Understand:

> You don't have to be religious
> for your prayers to be effective.

Research shows that it's the act of praying itself—not who or what you pray to—that makes it work.

> The act of praying is actually
> the clear focus of intentional thought
> with the expectancy of a favorable response
> from a Power greater than we are.

Pray whenever, however and to whomever you choose.

Here are some suggestions that not only make good sense but also are generally considered helpful in making prayer effective.

a. Pray at a time and in a quiet place where you won't be disturbed.
b. Allow yourself to feel empathy, love and compassion for yourself or for whomever you are praying.
c. Pray with a complete expectation that your prayer is being answered and that the desired result is right now in the process of manifestation.

People often ask, "How often should I pray?" This depends on you and on the situation. Once (or even twice) a day is the most common practice, but in a critical situation, three or more times a day is not unusual. The key, however, is to move out of prayer and back into the stream of everyday life with an expectancy that all is well.

For those of you who do not already follow an established way of praying or who might be interested in knowing more about my own personal prayer practice, I follow a general outline that differs from traditional prayer in that it is not a supplicating form of request but rather a mental directive. It is generally called "affirmative prayer" or "spiritual mind treatment." It is also known as "scientific prayer" or "prayer/treatment."

I find it is very helpful for me to speak my affirmative prayer out loud. I do this primarily for two reasons: (1) It helps me clarify my thinking, and (2) it helps me stay focused. As I do so, I say the words with feeling and think about them as I speak. I like to hear the sound of the words and feel the emotion that accompanies them.

The general guide that follows does not necessarily incorporate the exact words that I use, but rather the ideas that I recognize and affirm:

1. There is one creative Power and Intelligence (I call it "God" or "Spirit") which created all there is. It is ever-present and ever-active, always creating.

    At this point, I sometimes focus also on the Universality and Absoluteness of the Power, the Infinitude of the Intelligence and the Unconditional Love of this Presence. I often remind myself of the awesome vastness, balance and harmony of the universe in which we live and reflect to myself that the very Power and Intelligence that created it all is the same Power and Intelligence that is right now responding to my request.

2. I am one with this Power and Intelligence, and know that It is responsive to the direction of my thought and of my word. (If I am speaking my word for another, at this point I mention

their name and affirm the unity of both of us with each other and with the One Source.)

It is helpful for me to remind myself that this Presence, which I call "Spirit," is not somewhere far off. It is right where I am. It is working for me by working through me. It is always responsive because that is Its very nature.

3. This Power and Intelligence operates always for the greatest and highest good of all concerned.

This is called the "Law of Harmony," and I affirm it in every prayer/treatment I do. I do not have to worry about manipulation because by Its very nature Spirit always operates in balance and harmony. This helps me clarify that I am coming from a pure heart and that I know my good comes from an absolutely unlimited Source.

4. At this point, I clearly specify what it is that I desire, either for myself or another.

I am always careful to state my desire only in a positive way. For example, I would not say, "I do not want to lose my job." Instead, I would say, "I know that I am in my perfect job at all times." This opens the door for something to happen so that my current job becomes "my perfect job." Or maybe a transfer will accomplish that. Or possibly the best thing for me is to leave my current job and move to another job which will be "my perfect job."

Additionally, I try to be as clear as I can be, focusing always on the "what" and not the "how." In many cases, I add the words "this or better" after specifying my desire. I do this because my human intelligence is finite, but the Intelligence with which I am now communicating is Infinite and may well be able to guide and direct me to something better than what I am currently specifying. By adding these words, I declare my desire for, and openness and receptivity to, the very best.

At this point, I find that it is very helpful to take a few special moments of my prayer time to visualize my completed demonstration—to put myself right in it, to feel it, to experience it.

5. I affirm my belief that there is nothing anywhere to oppose this desire, and I reject and release anything in consciousness that might oppose or contradict this.

For me, this does two things. First, it adds to my conviction and faith in my spiritual mind treat-

ment. Second, I consciously erase any vestiges of my own negativity or anything in the collective consciousness of the human race that might conflict with this prayer/treatment. I am consciously and intentionally speaking my word in a way that is more powerful than any other.

6. I re-affirm whatever it is that I desire.

   This reaffirmation is usually brief, but I like to bring in my desire again as I am coming to the end of my prayer/treatment.

7. I give thanks and rejoice in the wonderful manifestation of this prayer/treatment in my world (or the world of whomever I am praying for).

   I end by recognizing that the "spiritual prototype" for my desire is now complete in the Mind of God. I am able to give thanks for it because I know it is complete in the invisible or Absolute realm, and it is now in the process of moving into perfect manifestation. I turn it over to Spirit with appreciation and joy, accepting the thing as done without any further concern on my part. In other words, I let go and let God.

And when I say, "Let go and let God," I mean exactly that. Whenever you have done an affirmative prayer, at that point your job in the creative process is complete. From there on, it is up to Spirit. Your continuing work is to guard your thinking. If you find yourself going down a path of negativity (and, admittedly, it's often hard not to), then you want to immediately get your thinking back on track.

Learn to make your thinking correspond
with your desires, and not with your fears.

Most of us will probably never reach a point where we don't have negative thoughts. They come and they go. They don't stay unless we invite them to and give them support. Don't let yourself worry about them. Let them come and let them go. Also, remember to tell yourself, "Cancel! Cancel!" and then replace the negative with a positive affirmation.

Your job is also to do what can only be done by you. And you will be guided to know what that is, and you will be guided to make the right choices. And, very often, it's not until later that we can see how perfectly everything worked out— for everyone!

Remember, in affirmative prayer (much as in visualization), your job is to specify clearly what you want and not what you don't want. You should state the key elements of your desire(s) and leave it up to Spirit (God, Universal Power) to fulfill your desire(s) in the way that is for your greatest and highest good as well as that of everyone else involved.

It is important to note that creatively praying a few times a day is a major key to success in obtaining your desires. There is no one to impress except your own consciousness, and once you have clearly impressed your desire on your consciousness (which is one with the Universal Mind of Spirit), your miracle is on its way. In other words, you have done your part, and now it's up to Spirit!

When you use this method of prayer for obtaining your desires, you will find that the more you do this work, the more you will realize that, with God, all things are possible and, further, that all things are always working for your greatest and highest good.

AFFIRMATIVE PRAYER

There is One Power, One Presence, One Creative Intelligence—Spirit, God—the Source of all there is. This One is Limitless Potentiality, and It lives in and through all that It creates. It is centered in me now, and responds perfectly to the impress of my thought and the direction of my word. I give great thanks for my ever-increasing awareness of this Truth.

Because Spirit, by Its very nature, can know only Good, It always operates for the greatest and highest good of all concerned. This means that my good does not depend on any particular person or circumstance, nor does it ever come at the expense of another.

I am alive with the very Life of God and give great thanks for the manifestation of This Life as perfect health. Any "healing" is simply the revealing of the greater Truth of my being, and I open to it now.

Since I am one with the Source of unlimited abundance, with joyous expectancy I open to a marvelous flow of abundance—of money and all good things. I am Divinely guided into paths of greater abundance in every area of my life.

I know that Unity and Harmony already exist at the Spiritual level of all life, so I open to and give thanks for the manifestation of these qualities in all my relationships.

The Infinite Intelligence of God guides and directs me to wonderful and harmonious solutions to any problems or challenges I may encounter, and the Law of Attraction draws to me all that I need—and more.

I know that the Universe never withholds Its Good; therefore, nothing can interfere with the perfect manifestation of the good that I desire. So, I joyously accept the good that I desire. I give great thanks for it, and I let it be so. And so it is.

CHAPTER 7

MIRACLES IN HEALTH AND MIRACLES IN SUCCESS

IN addition to the thinking that leads to miracles discussed in the last chapter, there are some specific guidelines concerning each of the four primary areas of desire that can help expand your consciousness to allow the miracle Power to express in your life. We'll cover two of those areas in this chapter, and the rest in Chapter 8.

Your part in the miracle-making process is a constant flow of positive, life-enhancing thoughts, including the feelings and emotions that go along with them.

Remind yourself that miracles happen.

They happen all the time. And if miracles ever happen, they can happen for you.

**Miracles happen because
of a changed consciousness.**

As you are probably beginning to recognize, it can take a lot of persistent work to change negative beliefs. It helps to remember that when our thinking is positive, we are working with the hidden laws of the universe in a positive way. We are working *with* the natural impulse of Life Itself, which is to express more of Itself, and to always express in balance and harmony.

Also, keep in mind that positive thought is in harmony with the Universal qualities of Spirit. Negative thought is in opposition to harmonious balance. Therefore:

Positive thought is more powerful than negative thought.

And, since we're talking about intentional and consciously consistent positive thought, we're talking about trained thought (page 103).

Trained thought is more powerful than untrained thought.

As we have already discussed, constructive thinking is more powerful than destructive thinking. This is because constructive thought is congruent with the nature of Spirit Itself and destructive thinking is not. With our positive thoughts, we place ourselves directly in the flow of Universal Power.

Some very dramatic research that relates to this has been done by Dr. Masaru Emoto, a Japanese scientist who has found that water is incredibly responsive to human consciousness. In *The Hidden Messages in Water,* Emoto reports on his ten years of photographing ice crystals. He was astounded when, in his earliest efforts, music by

Beethoven, Mozart and Chopin resulted in beautiful, well-formed crystals filled with lovely harmonious detail. Heavy-metal music, however, resulted in crystals that were fragmented and deformed.

Emoto's experiments also have included writing words or phrases such as "Thank you" and "Fool" on pieces of paper, which were then wrapped around identical bottles of water taken from the same source. Amazingly, and contrary to all logic, the water exposed to the phrase "Thank you" produced beautiful and harmonious ice crystals, while the water exposed to the word "Fool" produced malformed, fragmented crystals. Equally amazing, the same results were obtained even when these words and phrases were written in different languages.

Emoto states that, "The vibration of good words has a positive effect on our world whereas the vibration of negative words has the power to destroy."[1] Since the adult human body is composed of 70% water, this is well worth thinking about the next time we are tempted to put ourselves down. It's also very significant in terms of thinking about our physical health.

MIRACLES—IN HEALTH

Everything we do in life is either enhanced or diminished by the state of our health, and although the world is becoming increasingly aware of what is commonly called the "mind-body connection," few people understand just what this means and what it involves. Essentially, it means that the general state of our health is directly related to our consciousness, and further, a change in our health, *for better or worse*, involves a change in our consciousness.

In restoring the body to health, the most important things to always keep in mind are these:

1. Health is our natural state.

The healing Power we look for is already present within each one of us.

What really happens when our health diminishes or fails in some area is not that something has happened to us from the outside, but rather, something has happened to us from the *inside*. The Love, Power and Intelligence that created us continues to support us every moment, but, in some way, we have unintentionally and unwittingly limited it, restricted it or distorted Its flow by negative beliefs and thoughts—by our fears, by our anger, resentment and/or guilt.

Even our everyday lives are filled with indications of this. As a very simple example, if somebody says, "Boo!" behind us, we usually have a sharp intake of breath, our breathing becomes momentarily shallow, our blood pressure rises and it may take a few minutes before our bodies feel normal again. Was it the "Boo!" or was it our mental reaction to the "Boo!" that caused the bodily reaction? It was the reaction, of course. If we were deaf and didn't hear the "Boo!," there wouldn't have been any response. This is an almost absurdly small illustration, but the principle is the same. It's not the conditions and experiences of our lives that affect us, it's our perception, belief and reaction to those conditions and experiences that keep us healthy or allow disease and illness to manifest.

As we go about our daily lives, our bodies are constantly renewing themselves. The lining of the stomach renews itself in a week. The skin is entirely replaced in a month. The liver is regenerated in six weeks.[2] Indeed, *ninety-eight percent* of the atoms in our bodies are replaced annually.[3]

What this clearly tells us is that the very cells which are causing distress or disease in our bodies are constantly replacing themselves—and that those replacement cells *can* be healthy ones. Once there has been deterioration in our body, it doesn't have to be permanent, and it doesn't *have* to be progressive. It can go the other way, back to our natural state of health.

The most exciting part of this is that *the very process that allows for the deterioration of organs and systems in the first place is the same process that allows them to heal.* This means that our consciousness and beliefs can affect the regeneration of cells and organs positively or negatively. (If our consciousness remains unchanged, the progress of the disease or disorder continues in the same direction.)

2. See yourself healthy.

Regardless of whatever may be going on with you physically, remember what it feels like to be strong and energetic. Know that this healthy state of being is your natural state—your divine heritage.

As you think about yourself and your future, see yourself brimming with good health, energy and vitality.

Recognize that whatever you are experiencing at this moment is in a state of change, and that your body is in the process of reestablishing itself in balance and harmony.

The power of positive emotions has been known and written about for years. Some of the most exciting recent work in this area has been done at the Institute for HeartMath® in Boulder Creek, California. Their studies have shown that when we feel frustration, the pattern of our heart's rhythm becomes disordered, or "incoherent," whereas feelings of appreciation, love, compassion and other positive emotions produce a highly ordered or coherent pattern in the heart rhythms, reflecting greater synchronization of the two branches of our autonomic nervous system (which regulate 90% of the body's functions) as well as greater synchronization between the brain and heart, enabling them to work together to produce a single, coherent heart rhythm.[4] This is very important, because the electromagnetic field produced by our heart permeates every cell in our body.[5]

What these two findings indicate, of course, is that anxiety, frustration, anger and other stressful emotions directly affect not only the rhythm of the heart but, also to some extent, every cell in our bodies.

3. The healing Power operates by Law and not by caprice. You are never being punished with disease or illness by an angry deity, nor is your healing ever dispensed by caprice or favor.

Actually, I don't especially like the word "heal" because that makes it sound like there's something wrong that has to get fixed. Health is the natural state of your body, and since the body has an essential state of normal, healthy functioning, I prefer to think of what is considered "healing" to be "letting go of whatever doesn't belong" so that the healthy operation of the body is free to reveal itself. The more fully you are able to position yourself in the "flow of Life," the more fully you open to the balancing and harmonizing flow of Spirit in restoring your healthy functioning.

Sometimes, the demonstration of good health can be amazingly rapid. Larry's story is one such example.

Larry is a self-employed construction worker who has great faith in these principles, is well trained in them and has used them successfully in his life for years. He is very strong and muscular and has enjoyed good health most of his life. Driving home one evening, however, he began to experience rather frightening chest pains, so he drove to the emergency room of a local hospital. The echocardiogram and stress test he was given showed blockage in the lower part of his heart. Because there was no heart damage and there did not appear to be any imminent problem, Larry was released, but he was also scheduled for an angiogram and possible angioplasty two days later.

The next evening, Larry and I spent a long time on the phone, maybe two hours. Larry told me that for almost a year, his small business had been experiencing serious financial problems; this, in turn, had led to marital stress. His wife was planning to leave him. All areas of his life appeared to be blocked and in trouble. His business, finances, marriage and health all were all in a state of turmoil.

Larry realized that for months, rather than focusing on what he wanted in his world, his thinking had been focused only on his problems—going over them and over them, magnifying them, dissecting them and giving them great power. (This, too, is "squirrel-caging.") Rather than focusing his thoughts, energies and efforts on developing new business for his company, Larry had been angry and resentful over some disputed contracts, fearful of what would happen if they didn't work out the way he wanted. Rather than recognizing that his wife was also experiencing anxiety and stress, he was angry with her and resentful about what he saw as her disloyalty and lack of confidence in him.

We talked about all of this and discussed better ways of looking at these conditions and circumstances. Certainly we have to handle the issues in our lives, but we don't have to dwell on our problems and mentally grind away at them for twenty-four hours a day. But Larry *had* been grinding away at them with a combination of anger, resentment and fear—three of the most powerful negative emotions.

In a critical situation, we may very well feel as though we have no choice but to think about our problem all the time. We may even feel that in some way our worrying will help turn things around. But worry doesn't really help anything, and we do have a choice of what to think.

As Larry and I talked, Larry began to get a handle on his thinking and also his attitude toward the future of both his business and his marriage. He began to see that his anger and resentment about his business was only hurting him. He recognized that his fear was standing in the way of his moving forward. And he also realized that his wife was probably reflecting his negative emotions.

After we talked, we prayed.

Larry checked into the hospital the following morning for his angiogram and possible angioplasty. Amazingly, however, when they did the angiogram, there was no evidence of the blockage which had been captured *on film* just two days earlier. They did more tests, pronounced him fit and sent him home. On a follow-up visit with the doctor, Larry asked what had happened. The doctor mumbled something Larry couldn't quite make out and quickly changed the subject.

When it comes to Kurt, the demonstration of good health took longer. But Kurt's story also demonstrates another important aspect of spiritual healing (and, of course, it's all spiritual):

Principle is not bound by precedent.

You see, while a medical diagnosis is based on some combination of currently-existing factual data and expectation arising from historical data, spiritual healing is never bound by its historical pattern. Spiritual healing is, however, limited by our own expectation.

Kurt was twenty-seven when he first came to see me. He was one very sick man when he walked through the door. He weighed only 95 pounds (down from 140) and had been diagnosed with AIDS about eight months earlier. His face had an unhealthy pallor, and his eyes were sad and haunted. Kurt's family didn't know that he was sick. They didn't even know that he was gay, and Kurt didn't want them to find out.

His relationship with his father had always been painful for both of them. His father was an athlete and had been very disappointed when his slender, artistic son told the family he wanted to be a dancer. Kurt referred to his father as a "gay-basher" who, during Kurt's youth, made many comments that made Kurt feel like a really bad person. After a number of conversations Kurt came to recognize that he actually felt he deserved this disease as punishment for his lifestyle.

> It isn't what is going on in our lives that creates the stress in our bodies. Rather, it's what's going on in our minds.

Kurt was like a sponge when he began to understand a new way of looking at life in general and at himself in particular. The first realization he had was that his illness might not be, as he put it, a "death sentence." He came to accept that the Power, Intelligence and Love that created him was present, right where he was, and that It was capable of healing that which It had created.

He came to understand, too, that he was not being punished for his lifestyle but rather that he was experiencing the effects of blocking the flow of this Power and Intelligence in his life.

Kurt came to understand that if he was going to take responsibility for his own life, he had to be free to make his own decisions and choices. He began to see that it was actually necessary for him to make his own choices in life in order to express his own unique desires and talents. This understanding meant, however, that his father also had a right to his to his own opinions even if they reflected what both Kurt and I felt were narrow and restrictive beliefs.

Most importantly, perhaps, Kurt came to know that he was not a bad person.

He came to understand that he was a divine creation of an Infinite and Loving Creator and that the Power and Intelligence that created him was expressing through him every moment. He came to know that the Spirit that created him is completely nonjudgmental and that the Love that created him is unconditional.

Kurt and I prayed together three times a week. In addition, he began using a very simple affirmation every day, "I *am* perfect health every day in every way." (Note: When someone says, "I am perfect health..." they are identifying with the perfect pattern in which each of us is created—in other words, the "above." Others are more comfortable saying, "I am *in* perfect health..." or, "I enjoy perfect health." If you choose to use this affirmation, use whichever style you're most comfortable with.)

He asked me how many times he should say this. "As often as you possibly can," I told him.

So, he said it out loud; he said it silently; he made up a little tune and he sang it; he whistled it. Later, he told me that he repeated this affirmation to himself literally hundreds of times a day. He became completely encompassed by this wonderful, life-giving idea. Slowly, but surely, he began to internalize the idea that he was expressing perfect health.

He thought about cyclist Lance Armstrong who recovered from a "terminal diagnosis" of testicular cancer that had spread to his lungs and his brain. Not only did he recover, but he continued with his love of bicycle racing and came in first, year after year after year, in the tortuous 2,100 mile Tour de France bicycle racing competition. Kurt knew that the same Creative Power that moved through Lance Armstrong in restoring his body to its natural state of health was also operating in his own body. He thought about that every day, and he knew that if it happened for Lance, it could happen for him, too.

Someone told Kurt about a wonderful nutritionist, and with the help of this nutritionist, he incorporated major changes in his diet. The nutritionist subsequently referred him to another doctor. This new doctor was a very positive man. He got Kurt exercising, and he even told him that *a death sentence is only a death sentence if you accept it.* This was the same thing I had told him. Kurt liked this idea a lot. He should: It reinforced everything he was doing.

One day as we were talking, Kurt looked up unexpectedly and said, "That's it! I want to talk to my father. I want to tell him that I'm gay." He arranged a visit home within the next week or so.

The next time we talked, Kurt had tears in his eyes as he recounted a very emotional visit. It turned out that his father had known for years that Kurt was gay. He told Kurt he was happy to be able to talk to him about it, and he apologized for all the hurtful things he had said throughout the years. He even admitted that some of them had been intentional, and he was ashamed and regretful about that. He assured Kurt that he had always loved him and would always be there for him.

Kurt, who had been feeling progressively stronger, started gaining weight. His new confidence and self-esteem became evident to everybody. Then, it was time for another blood test. Kurt went for the test, but had great trepidation about going to his new doctor's office for the results. He was feeling so good about everything in his life, and he was afraid the test results would ruin his new happiness. He asked me to go with him.

It was a beautiful Tuesday morning that we sat together in the doctor's office and heard the doctor say that as far as they could determine, not only was there no evidence of AIDS, *there was no trace of the HIV virus*. Even though the doctor had copies of Kurt's earlier blood tests which clearly showed the disease and its progression, he shook his head and wondered if it was all some sort of mistake.

For several years following that visit, Kurt continued to get semi-annual blood tests. There was never any further evidence of either AIDS or the HIV virus. The same Power and Intelligence that had restored Lance Armstrong to health had indeed done Its perfect job again—this time, for Kurt.*

Sometimes I talk with people and realize that they are simply unwilling to put forth the discipline and the mental and emotional energy that may be involved in changing consciousness. When I write this, please be clear—*we* don't restore the body to health. As I continue to point out in this book, our job is *to change consciousness*—to expand it to a higher level. We don't change the body; we change our thinking from negative to positive. It's the removal of these negative thoughts of limited health that allows the body to regain its natural state—which is health. But it does take discipline, and it does take mental and emotional energy.

---

* In her book *The Field*, investigative journalist Lynne McTaggart details several controlled scientific studies of the effects of prayer on Stage IV AIDS patients in which there were remarkable healing results.

One of the studies done at the Institute for HeartMath® demonstrated this dramatically. The study was done with twenty-eight researchers who had been trained how to generate a coherent state between the heart and the brain by maintaining positive emotions. Each was given a vial of human placenta DNA (the most pristine available) for the purpose of mentally influencing the sample. When these researchers maintained the coherent state, *the DNA responded by unwinding or winding, depending on the intention of the researcher. In other words it took both emotional coherence and focused intention to affect the DNA.*[*6] This clearly demonstrates the importance of sustaining positive emotions as well as focused intention.

When there is illness and disease, there is also mental and emotional energy moving in one direction or another.

Both Larry and Kurt reversed all their mental and emotional energy from negative channels to positive channels—and this is what allowed the healing to take place. Remember Sheldon in Chapter 5? When he made his decision not to go to the Mayo Clinic for surgery, that's what he did as well. He shifted his mental and emotional energy from negative to positive.

However, not only patients, but their loved ones too, spend large amounts of time and mental energy thinking either positively or negatively about the current and

---

* Note the similarity between the findings of Dr. Emoto in photographing the ice crystals and the Institute for Heartmath® in their studies with human placenta DNA. Both report strong positive responses to love, gratitude and appreciation.

future health of the patient. This was what Virginia in Chapter 4 did when her paralyzed daughter faced additional life-threatening surgery, and as you have seen, it can have life-enhancing results.

By the way, some people who believe in Spiritual healing do not believe in doctors. *I take no position about whether someone should or should not undergo surgery. I do believe that each person has an Inner Knower to guide and direct them in this important decision. The doctor and the surgeon are Spirit in action, too. To me, medical advances are in keeping with the natural expression of the Intelligence of Spirit, which is operating through new procedures and medical knowledge.*

The important thing in restoring our bodies to their natural state of health is that we need to be on guard constantly to keep our thinking focused on what we want and not on what we don't want. Remember:

**Power flows toward and magnifies
that to which we give our attention.**

MIRACLES—IN SUCCESS

Our primary purpose in being is to express life. Sometimes people may say that their purpose in life is to be happy, but:

**Happiness is not a goal.
It's a byproduct of living an expressed life.**

Think about it. The more fully-expressed the life, the greater the joy and happiness we experience. So, when we talk about success, we are really talking about successful *creative expression.*

When we are little children, we are constantly exploring, testing and growing. The experiences that result are often joyous ones. As we grow older, however, and for a myriad of reasons, this inherent desire to express and grow often becomes stifled. We put it aside in favor of the many other demands of our growing and maturation process.

Too often we think that because we have stifled this creative urge for so long, it's too late to follow our dream. Not so!

The ideas that beckon to us are really the Infinite announcing an invisible world of endless possibilities.

So whenever you start telling yourself that, "It's too late," "It just wouldn't work out" or any of the other reasons we give ourselves for not expressing these wonderful ideas we all have within ourselves, remind yourself that this invisible world of endless possibilities is also ready and waiting to support you in your efforts.

Philosopher David Henry Thoreau wrote, "Most men lead lives of quiet desperation." This may have been true back in the nineteenth century, but it doesn't have to be true for anyone. Not today! Not any more! Nobody *needs* to lead a life of quiet desperation. We are created to express ourselves, to live with purpose and to enjoy doing it. Today we are learning how to change our lives. We are able to move from desperation to wonderfully balanced, rewarding and fulfilled lives.

Hundreds of years ago, the Sufi poet Rumi wrote:

"I have spent my time stringing
and unstringing my instrument while
the song I came to sing remains unsung."

Each one of us is a unique individualization of an Infinite Creator, and, therefore, we each have our own song to sing. *If we don't sing it, it just won't get sung, because nobody else can sing it.*

Our creative expression, our success, is essentially what we choose to do with our lives, and it's a very broad category. It includes our professional or business life, which we frequently use as a "measure of our success." It also means the way we spend our discretionary time and our unique artistic expression, whether via music, writing, dancing, etc. It means doing the things that make us feel most alive. For some, this might mean dedication to one life-long creative expression (such as Picasso, painter and sculptor.) Someone else (such as Leonardo da Vinci, painter, sculptor, architect, engineer, musician, scientist and philosopher) might pursue a number of different paths almost concurrently. And someone else (such as Grandma Moses, who began painting in her nineties) might begin to express a completely new interest or talent quite late in life. The point here is that all of these interests are good, and if we truly have the desire to express ourselves in a particular area, it's possible to do so. We can pursue whatever interests we choose, and know that we are fully supported by Spirit.

All our desires and interests are simply indications of the infinitude of Spirit expressing through us.

All too often, we think that if only outer circumstances would change, we could be happy. The reverse is true: The change on the inside is what needs to take place.

Buckminster Fuller said, "The minute you begin to do what you really want to do, it's really a different kind of life."[7] Whether it's your business life or your leisure time, remember:

Your soul wants to sing.

When we are living a life in which our soul does not sing enough, all sorts of things go wrong—in all areas of our lives. We are all here to live and enjoy living. Your business or professional life can and should be richly rewarding. If it's not, something is wrong, but it's something that you can change.

In addition to the mental attitudes discussed in the last chapter, there are some important caveats regarding success.

1. Place no blame.

This means that to be successful, you must take responsibility for your own life. This is not always easy to do, especially when there are problems. When we run into problems, we frequently look at the circumstances and say, "If only... ," followed by wherever we're placing the blame. The important thing is to remember that whatever is happening on the outside is not the problem. For example, the moment you see your problems or lack of success as being the fault of someone or something else, you have placed the responsibility for your life with another person or some outside circumstance. In your mind, you have become either a victim of circumstances or a victim of the actions of somebody else.

Wherever you place the blame, you are also placing the responsibility and control for your life and your success.

Think further about what this means in terms of a Universe that responds to our thoughts and beliefs. When you believe someone else is responsible for your problems, then that person, group of people or set of circumstances becomes the power in your life. They, and not you, have control over your life. Worse yet, you establish thought patterns and beliefs that continue to attract into your life people and things that create problems for you, and circumstances in which you feel victimized.

If you want to be in control of your own life, you need to take responsibility for what is happening in it. This can be difficult to do, so remind yourself, *if you don't control it, you can't change it.*

2. Check your attitude.

Do you really love what you are doing? Do you at least *like* what you're doing?

If you don't enjoy what you're doing, you're likely to move from one set of problems to another. As soon as one thing is taken care of, another problem will appear. I'm not talking about the normal challenges to be expected in your work. I'm talking about problems that make your work distasteful and unrewarding. Very simply, if you aren't enjoying *most* of the hours you spend doing whatever it is you are doing, then you're not very happy during those hours. And if you are not very happy most of the time, your thoughts and thought patterns during that period of time (and for most of us, it constitutes a lot of our time) are not very happy either. And of course, when your thought patterns are negative, you are creating a field of negativity that is actively drawing negative experiences into your world. In fact:

This negativity affects not only your business or profession, but also your health, working relationships and personal relationships.

If you are working at a job you don't enjoy and you don't change either your job or your attitude, you may very well find the choice is taken out of your hands. Life never stands still.

A man I knew quite well called me for guidance because his life had become a shambles. About six months earlier, he had been seriously injured in an automobile accident. In order to hold his job for him, his company required written verification of his physical condition within thirty days. Somehow, despite repeated reminders, there was a slip-up, and the notice wasn't received in time. Even though this man had been with the company over ten years, they refused to reinstate him.

This man was outraged that his company was treating him so callously. "Did you like your job?" I asked. "Like it? I *hated* it!" he responded. "I couldn't wait to get out of there." Well, he was out of there all right, but not on his terms... and not in a way that was doing him any good.

You are the one responsible—and the only one responsible—for your attitude.

Some years ago, a young man in northwestern Illinois grew up playing and loving baseball. He even had great dreams of being a professional athlete. But, one day at the shoe factory where he worked, he had an accident and lost the top joint of his middle finger. In that moment, his dreams of athletic competition were ended. Reluctantly, he began working for a local drugstore to prepare himself for a career as a pharmacist.

But filling orders and cashiering were tedious and unrewarding. There were no cheers, no applause, no excitement. Besides that, he wasn't even paid very much. Shortly after the end of his first year of employment, he left.

The lure of the big city drew him to Chicago, but what should he do? The only thing he knew was the drug store/pharmacy business, but his last experience was far from a positive one and he didn't want that again. So, this time he determined to dedicate himself to making the work interesting and rewarding. For the next seven years, this man worked for several of Chicago's finest pharmacies. He learned what they did right; he learned what they did wrong; and he devoted himself to making these pharmacies better whenever he could.

The more dedicated he became, the more challenged he was to build a store of outstanding service and quality. He became so absorbed that he knew he had to buy his own store in order to put into practice all the innovative ideas that kept coming to him.

So, Charles R. Walgreen, Sr. bought his first drug store in 1901. Twelve years later, there were four stores; eight years after that, twenty. By 1930 there were 525 stores, and by the time of his death in 1939, his superb planning and vision had established the principles upon which the company continued to flourish well into the next century (at which time the company was growing at the rate of more than 450 stores a year).

All this came from a change in attitude!

There are two other interesting aspects to the story of Charles R. Walgreen. First, remember that he had to give up his dream of being a professional athlete because as long as he clung to his "lost dream," his innate organizational and visionary abilities were stifled. As he became more and more involved in what he was doing, however, he became enthused and excited and began devising new and innovative ways of improving business. As this happened, the result was an exponential growth in the expression of his own capabilities and talents as well as his business.

The second interesting aside on this story is that even during the Great Depression of the 1930's, Charles R. Walgreen adopted major philanthropy as a corporate as well as personal mission. Walgreens was one of the very first American companies to establish pension and profit sharing for its employees. The initial contribution of $500,000 to this corporate program was a personal contribution by Mr. Walgreen. Additionally, the company itself contributed hundreds of thousands of dollars to the University of Chicago—during the Depression as well![8] The reality is inescapable:

> Spiritual flow is synergistically expanded and multiplied when we allow ourselves to operate generously and unselfishly in whatever we are doing.

The reverse is also true (as was evidenced by the young man who was in the automobile accident and lost his job). When we are blocking the flow of Spirit, those results, too, are expanded and multiplied.

We are one with *unlimited potentiality.* This is a concept that we don't easily grasp, but the more we are able to open to it, the greater our awareness of this Truth becomes. And as this happens, our creative expression expands—exponentially!

Our highest vision for ourselves is only a limited idea when compared to the greatness of our spiritual potential.

The Law of Attraction brings into our lives the right people at the right time. The door opens for us at just the right place. We find new talents and resources within ourselves beyond what we had ever expected. And we find ourselves living our lives with greater love and joy and peace and enthusiasm than we had ever imagined. This happens when we are we open to a greater and higher expression of life and are willing to do what we need to do—when we pour our energies, our enthusiasm and ourselves expectantly into whatever it is that we are doing.

3. Even our bodies respond to our desire to express creatively.

Few of us realize the extent to which our physical and creative limitations exist in our minds. As an example, competitive running is one of mankind's oldest sports. Runners probably competed with each other in prehistoric times, but it was not until 1855, with the design of the chronograph, that we could accurately time runners and know not only who won, but also how fast they ran. And they could run fast—a little over a mile in four minutes. But, they never did so in less than four minutes. In fact, it was thought that it might be a physical impossibility for anyone to ever run a mile in less than four minutes.

Then, ninety-nine years later, along came Roger Bannister. On May 6, 1954, at Oxford, England, he became the first man in history to break the four-minute mile when he ran one mile in 3:59.4. Just over one month later, another runner broke the four-minute mile—and then another, and another. Today, every good miler is able to break the four-minute mile. The belief has changed... and so has the physical capability of the runners.

They can because they *think* they can!

Just as runners had a mental block and could not break the four-minute mile, the same thing was true for weightlifters. At first, nobody could ever lift 500 pounds. They could lift 497—they could lift 498—and they could even lift 499. But nobody could ever lift 500 pounds.

Then, in the 1970 World Weightlifting Championship, Vasili Alexeyev called for 499 pounds, which happened to be the world record. They gave him the weights, and he went through his lift successfully. Then, following regulations, they re-weighed the weights. Lo and behold, the first weighing had been incorrect. The weights did not weigh 499; they actually weighed 501-1/2 pounds. He had

broken the world's record by 2-1/2 pounds! This phenom-
enal feat was quickly repeated *six more times in the next
six months.*

Belief opens the door to allow
the Power to flow through us.

Too many of us think harshly about our bodies, and
yet it is proven again and again that our bodies also
respond to our appreciation of them and our expectation
that they will perform well.

The next story that follows illustrates how wonderfully our bodies respond to our desire to express creatively. (And, by inference, it illustrates the importance of
always valuing and treasuring our physical bodies.)

Jeff taught music at a local high school. He loved
music and, in addition to frequent "gigs" with traveling
bands, he was honored to play occasionally with the
Chicago Symphony Orchestra. His primary instrument
was the trumpet. Jeff was an outstanding sight-reader but
found the very high notes were challenging for him (as
they are for most trumpet players.)

Although Jeff worked for years to improve his range, as
he approached B below high C, he was unable to sustain
the note without cracking. This affected the number of
opportunities he had to play with the Symphony
Orchestra. Additionally, hitting the high notes was also
very important for him when he was featured during his
gigs with the bands. Jeff had all but given up before he

came to see if I could help him improve by "even half a tone."

Early in the first conversation, it was obvious that Jeff was really hard on himself—angry with himself generally, and with his lips and his breath specifically for not being able to move through this "block."

What we did was simple. I suggested that rather than feel angry at his lips, he begin to love them. And he did. He began to love his whole body, but especially his lips. Many times a day, he said to himself:

"I love myself. I love my body. I especially love my lips."

Within thirty days, his playing had dramatically changed. First, he was able to easily hit B below high C... then C, then C sharp, and finally even D. Two and one-half tones more in thirty days! *And* he was able to sustain clear, sweet notes. This is an extraordinary degree of proficiency achieved by the finest of trumpet players, such as Doc Severinson and Maynard Ferguson.

When the "I can" consciousness replaces the "I can't" consciousness—you can and you will!

The next part of Jeff's story illustrates something else that happens with miracles.

Not only did Jeff receive all the additional bookings that he had wanted, he also was named director of the music department at the school where he taught.

Interestingly, he also got the courage to begin dating a young lady he had been interested in for months—and within another few months, they were married. Shortly after that, they bought a lovely new home.

These were things Jeff had wanted for years, but they "simply never happened."

As we expand consciousness and grow in one area, more often than not we open up and grow in other areas as well.

The moment Spirit has an opportunity for greater expression through us, It moves right into action. When we put positive ideas into our consciousness, the Infinite multiplies them and takes them to a manifestation beyond anything we would have imagined.

One final thought with respect to creative expression:

Our desire to express is actually Spirit Itself desiring expression through us.

The wonderful and exciting ideas and urges that we get that make us want to move forward in new and different ways are actually coming from a Higher Source. This also means that when we first become aware of our desire or our idea for greater expression, the idea or the desire is *already supported by Spirit.* Everything necessary for the fulfillment of the idea already exists and is ready for unfoldment whenever we are ready and begin doing whatever is necessary for us to do.

Whatever you can do,
or dream you can,
Begin it.
Boldness has genius, power,
and magic in it.
—JOHANN WOLFGANG VON GOETHE

CHAPTER 8

MIRACLES IN PROSPERITY AND MIRACLES IN RELATIONSHIPS

MIRACLES—IN PROSPERITY

DOESN'T it seem as though money just flows to some people while others can't buy a five-dollar bill for six dollars? What most people don't understand is that this isn't about luck, it's about consciousness!

Prosperity, abundance and money are all tied together in the minds of most of us. One of the best definitions of prosperity I have heard came from Dr. Raymond Charles Barker, author of *Treat Yourself to Life,* who said:

"I define prosperity as *the ability* to do what you want to do at the instant you want to do it."[1]

In order to have miracles in prosperity and abundance, we need to feel good about ourselves, and we need to feel good about money. Money is important. We all depend on it, and in one way or another, we use it or make use of it every day.

Most of our basic ideas about money, abundance and prosperity come from our childhood. They're concepts of long-standing. They come from ideas that our parents, siblings, family and friends held and expressed and talked about that we simply adopted as "true."

Not only are they often *un*true, they may even be misstated! Here's an example. People often say, "Money is the root of all evil." The correct quote is, "The *love* of money is the root of all evil," referring, of course, to greediness rather than the appropriate enjoyment of abundance and prosperity. Quite a difference, don't you agree?

In developing a consciousness that attracts greater prosperity, the following points are important.

1. Know that you are worthy and deserving.

I recall one young man who spent a large part of his life always struggling to meet the monthly bills. He had an excellent education, was extremely bright and capable, and always earned a very high income. But it seemed that no matter how much money he earned, it was never enough.

As this young man began to understand the principles of prosperity, he realized that since childhood he had been practically haunted by the memory of a postcard he received from his father one year when he was a little boy attending camp. The early lines of the postcard are lost to memory, but the lines that stood out were this: "Do you still have any money left? Your mother tells me money burns a hole in your pocket." From that time on, this man saw himself as someone who simply couldn't keep from spending far more than he earned.

It was many years later before he finally began to see himself as a financially responsible person and his finances began to turn around. Interestingly, prior to changing his self-image, he had one unfortunate experience after another where he "just missed out" on situations that would have resulted in a lot of income to him. But after he began to see himself as a financially responsible person, many things changed in his life. Not only did he always seem to have the money he needed, but excellent financial opportunities presented themselves as he restructured his financial world.

You are worthy and deserving because that is your Spiritual heritage. You didn't have to "earn it." It is your Spiritual birthright.

Any ideas you may have to the contrary are the result of false ideas given to you by others.

2. There is One Source, but many channels. The Source is always providing for us.

The reason this principle is so important is that we have a natural tendency to confuse "the channel" with "the Source." The Source is exactly that—the Source of all supply, the Source of everything, God, Higher Power, Universal Power, Creative Intelligence. The channel is exactly that—a channel of supply through which the Source operates.

The Source is Spirit, and the channel is the particular area through which the supply provided by the Source is currently flowing. The channels are your job, your investments or anything else that brings prosperity into your world. The key is to know that the Source will always provide, if not through one channel, then through another and often better or more appropriate channel.

We are one with the One Source of supply, and It is always expressing through us based on what we expect—truly expect—to have happen.

The importance of this is to know that there is no need to hold on fearfully to one channel of supply. When we do this, we are simply creating a fear of loss. We need to remind ourselves:

When one door closes, another door opens.

This is true in prosperity, opportunity and relationships. When one channel of supply "dries up" (whether it's a job or a client) it simply allows another door to open. It's important for us to know this and to let go of fear. Easier said than done, I know, but the point here is to focus on what you want, not on what you don't want.

Gail's story is a marvelous example. Gail was an illustrator for a large department store, and she was very talented. She could do sketches that really brought the clothes to life—even when there were no models to work from. She loved illustration work, but she felt she was unappreciated, overworked and underpaid. And besides being poorly paid, she didn't even get paid overtime—of which there was a lot!

Gail really didn't appreciate much of anything about her life when we first began working together. She didn't feel gratitude for herself, her job, her talent or her life. She really didn't appreciate anything.

One of the first things I asked Gail to do was to write a series of letters—letters of appreciation. This encouraged her to look at her life and recognize that there was much there to appreciate.

She began by appreciating her parents and the good things about her childhood. Then she began appreciating the good things about her job, herself, her life and her outstanding talent.

Gail read the letters aloud to me each week after she wrote them. And then, as she felt moved to do so, she would read them to herself at home.

Slowly but surely Gail's attitude changed from one of anger and resentment to one of appreciation for all the good in her life.

One day Gail walked in, angry and upset. "They fired me," she railed. "Congratulations!" I responded. "Now you really can allow your talent to be expressed and appreciated."

It didn't take Gail long to see her situation in a new light. That same day she went out and had business cards printed. She began calling every company and advertising agency she knew to let them know of her availability and to set appointments to show them her portfolio. She was delighted that she was able to set up two such appointments early on.

To help her stay focused during that first year of freelancing, Gail wrote out powerful affirmations on 3" x 5" cards and read these out loud to herself several times every day. She even repeated these affirmations to herself silently throughout the day to further reinforce her positive thinking. These were her affirmations:

- I am successful in all that I do.
- I am appreciated and my work is appreciated.
- I am abundantly compensated for all that I do.
- I am divinely guided to the right people, and the right people are drawn to me.
- I am divinely guided as I embark on each new project.

Whenever she met with prospective clients who were dismissive of her work, she recognized that they were not the right people for her to work with. And that was okay. In fact, it was better than okay, because Gail realized she was better off spending her time looking for the right client than working with the wrong client.

At the end of the first year, Gail was amazed to realize that she had earned twice as much as she earned in her last year on her previous job. Yes, she had worked really hard, because in addition to her design work she was also building her client base, but she loved every minute of it. She was excited and invigorated about everything she was doing.

But that was only the beginning for Gail. At the end of the first year her work really took off. She developed a unique method of displaying her sketches in retail windows that made them look three-dimensional. Her innovative idea was very successful, and within five years, Gail was earning several hundred thousand dollars a year. She fully appreciated herself and her talent, and so did the people she worked with.

Miracles come from a change in consciousness, not a change in circumstances.

3. Make sure your intentions are pure.

Very simply, when we attempt to do good things for bad reasons, we set up a whole field of infinite "bad."

Far too often, people feel they need to take their good at the expense of someone else. This happens in many areas of life, but it seems to be especially predominant in financial matters. This comes from a "fear of lack," or a concern that there is not enough to go around.

Focus on lack of fear rather than fear of lack.

It is important to recognize that your good does not depend on taking something away from someone else. We are dealing with a Creative Intelligence and Power that does not need to take from one to give to another, and it is this Intelligence and Power that is at work bringing about that which you desire.

There is another important reason for being clear about your intentions.

> If you believe that you can only have your good by taking from someone else, then the other part of that same equation is that you are setting yourself up so that your own good is constantly at risk.

And, if you believe your own good is constantly at risk... well, I think you know the rest.

One of the most successful businessmen I know uses the following for both his personal and his business credo. It is a perfect expression of Spiritual harmony.

> If it's not good for me, it's not good for you; and,
> if it's not good for you, it's not good for me.

We've also all heard this adage:

> If you want to make money, find something
> you enjoy doing, and do it.

Abundance and prosperity flow most easily when we're doing something we love. When we're doing something we truly enjoy, there is lightheartedness and a joyfulness in everything we do. We feel fully alive. The Law of Attraction is working for us, drawing good things to us, and we are open to every opportunity that comes our way.

When we're doing something we don't enjoy, our heart is not in it, and everything related to what we're doing becomes drudgery.

Realize too, though, that many times, a change in attitude is possible, and, as we saw with Charles R. Walgreen, can bring life-changing results.

On the other hand, when we plow ahead and force ourselves into a field of endeavor which is not suited to either our interests, our training or our abilities, we usually find ourselves working very hard and we often end up attempting to manipulate circumstances and/or people. The reason is that we're using our willpower rather than our co-creative power, and it usually turns out to be hard and unrewarding work.

One of my colleagues, Karl, tells this story about himself.

When Karl was a young man, he was very much in love with a young lady whose father was one of the most successful men in the community. For some reason, this man didn't care very much for Karl and certainly didn't want him for a son-in-law. Karl became convinced that if he had a lot of money, the girl's father would change his mind.

Karl was an electrical engineer, and although he had a reasonably good job, he didn't really believe he could ever earn the kind of money he thought the father wanted for his daughter. He decided he needed to really hit it big in some different field.

Along came an opportunity that looked just like the golden opportunity Karl needed. He read about a sales opportunity that offered a virtual fortune for the right person. Although Karl had no sales experience, and despite the fact that he didn't even like the idea of sales, he was drawn to the idea of the big income this opportunity promised.

It took almost every penny Karl had saved, but he bought the rights to a seven-state territory in which he would sell plastic dishes to hospitals and schools. Now, at that time, plastic dishes were very new. They were a hot item, and Karl was convinced that he would make a fortune. Not only that, he was also convinced that once he had introduced these plastic dishes into all these institutions, the income would be self-generating. So not only would he be wealthy, but he would have lots of leisure time as well. Surely this would impress the young lady's father and change the man's mind about him.

Well, sales were good. In fact, they were really very good at first. Everybody who saw these dishes bought them. But pretty soon there were complaints. The quality of the dishes was good, but there was a problem with the cups. They stained. And within a very short period of time, all the cups were so stained that nobody wanted to use them. They might still be clean and sanitary, but they certainly didn't look like it! So not only did his customers not re-order as Karl had expected, but they began discontinuing their use of the dishes. Some even wanted their money back.

Now, this was not good. Karl didn't even like selling the dishes in the first place, and he now found that trying to handle the complaints was awful for him. He didn't know what to do, so he finally did the only thing he could think of: He advertised to sell his territorial rights to someone else. As he put it, all he wanted to do was to "cut my losses and get out!"

Karl was able to sell his rights to someone else without losing too much money on the whole deal because he minimized the customers' complaints and didn't tell prospective buyers about the stained cups. He felt really fortunate to get out of the business without having lost all of his investment.

The man who bought the territory found out about the stained cups soon enough, of course, and he was not happy about what he felt was Karl's misrepresentation. But this man *was* a good salesman. He loved selling, and to this man, handling complaints was part of the job. He essentially laughed and said, "It goes with the territory. If you can't handle the complaints, you shouldn't be in sales."

Nevertheless, he *did* have a problem—the unhappy customers were still unhappy. This man, however, took a completely different attitude than Karl. One of his favorite sayings was this:

The opposite end of the problem is the solution.

This man was convinced that every problem has a good solution. (Notice that while he acknowledged the problem as a fact, he focused on the *solution*.) He gave the matter a lot of thought and talked to a lot of people about how he might offer these terrific plastic dishes without their benefits being compromised by the fact that the cups would become stained with use. None of their suggestions seemed to be good solutions.

Then the answer came in a flash of inspiration. Why did the cups have to be made out of the same plastic material as the rest of the dishes? What if the cups were the same color, but made out of some other strong material that would not stain? He went to a manufacturer who made porcelain dishes and arranged to have some heavy porcelain mugs made. Then he contacted all of his customers and offered a free replacement of the stained plastic cups (and saucers, in some cases) with the heavy mugs. Everyone loved his idea. Not only did the mugs not stain, but most people enjoyed drinking out of them even more than they did the cups.

The end of the story is that there truly *were* many millions of dollars to be made with these plastic dishes in that seven-state territory—but it was the second man, and not Karl, who became wealthy.

Karl had gone into this business for the wrong reasons—a lot of wrong reasons, in fact. He didn't know anything about selling; he was neither trained nor well-suited for it; and he was too focused on making a quick dollar to do the job the way it needed to be done. When a problem arose, *he was too focused on the problem to see the solution*.

Basically, then, whatever you are doing, do it because you enjoy it.

"Joy makes one porous to Spirit"*

And joyous activity opens our hearts and minds to the flow of Spirit in everything we undertake.

MIRACLES—IN RELATIONSHIPS

We all need relationships. We are relational beings, and in our relationships we can experience great joy. We can also experience great pain. What we want to try to do is to function as joyously as possible in our relationships and learn how to move away from those relationships that do not work. And, most importantly, we need to learn the difference.

A relationship does not "give us joy." We *experience* the relationship joyously.

Both joy and pain are in us and not in the relationship itself. It is important to know that we are not—or at least we don't have to be—victims in relationships any more than we need to be victims in other areas of life. We make choices, and we experience consequences.

As we discussed in the chapters on quantum physics:

At the invisible level, we are all interconnected.

---

* One of my mentors quoted this to me many years ago during a counseling session, and I have enjoyed using it for myself and others ever since. Regrettably, however, the name of the originator is lost in memory.

I think most people recognize that there is some kind of *vibrational*, or unspoken, communication possible between people. Studies at the Institute for HeartMath® indicate that the electromagnetic vibration from the heart can actually be measured from more than nine feet away. Some people may be better tuned in than others, but there is a vibrational connection in all relationships. The closer or more intimate the relationship, the more powerful that connection is and the more powerful its communication.

As I was writing this chapter, something happened that illustrates the powerful and mysterious way this connection can work, especially with those we love. I have a favorite casual restaurant where I often sit by the fireplace to do research and make notes. Over the years that I've gone there, I have become quite friendly with Cindy, the manager, and we often talk about these principles.

Cindy has an extremely full schedule. During the week she has a full-time job as an emergency room administrator in a local hospital and then on weekends she drives almost four hours round-trip to manage the restaurant Friday evenings and Saturdays.

One Saturday, Cindy came over to my table with a question. "I woke up this morning with a really strong feeling that I should take a day off and go visit my mother. She's 83 and in a retirement home and I haven't seen her for quite a while, but I talk to her all the time. What do you make of that?"

I told her that I thought it was very important to honor the feeling and to call her mother at the first opportunity to set a date to visit. From the way Cindy described the feeling she had, it seemed to be more than simply feeling guilty, and I told her so. But, even if it was simply a feeling of guilt, I told her it was important to not put off making the call.

The next day I got a call at home from Cindy. The story was astounding. Cindy had called her mother that same afternoon but had gotten her mother's voice mail. She left a message suggesting that her mother call back about 10 p.m. when she would be driving home and they could talk and make plans to see each other. Cindy, however, left work early that afternoon and was already at home before 10 p.m. She also accidentally left her cell phone in her car, so her mother wasn't able to reach her on her cell at 10 p.m. after all.

But what also happened was this. Her mother set her alarm for 10 p.m. and when the alarm went off, she used her bedside phone to return Cindy's call. There was no answer, but since she was now awake, Cindy's mother decided to use the washroom. As she tried to get out of bed, however, she found her left leg "wasn't working." She summoned help from the retirement home staff, and they, in turn, took her to the hospital where she was admitted with a transient ischemic accident (TIA).

The family later learned that one of the doctors had temporarily taken her mother off a powerful heart medication to treat another condition without the knowledge of the cardiologist who prescribed it. If Cindy's mother had not tried to get up when she did, she probably would not have been able to summon help later during the night, and most likely she would not have lived until morning.

Although we are not usually aware of it, this vibrational connection, this unspoken communication, is always taking place. I'm sure you've experienced this in your own life or you know someone who has.

> This vibrational communication is always taking place, and the more sensitive and honoring we become to our intuitive guidance, the more receptive we will be to this communication.

Yes, we are, essentially, relational beings. Think for a moment about the number and types of relationships we all have—parents, spouses or partners, children, siblings, aunts, uncles, cousins, bosses, co-workers, business associates, friends, neighbors, merchants, teachers, bus drivers and so on.

It is important to remember the following:

1. **As we change consciousness, the relationship will change.**

Every relationship we have is a "right" relationship based on our current consciousness. The relationship—as it is at any given time—reflects the qualities and limitations of both parties, their expectations of themselves and each other, and the interaction between the two parties. These expectations, however, often restrict one—or more often, both—parties from growing to their fullest self-expression.

In most cases, the single most important thing we can do to improve a relationship is this:

Let go of emotionally-based demands.

This means not trying to make someone conform to a mold that we have created for them or the relationship. This also means:

Let go of negative feelings about the other person.

Does this mean you have to like everything the other person does? No, of course not. You don't have to like what they do, and you don't even have to like them. Just don't *dis*like them. For example, you may have a completely different set of ethics, attitudes, preferences and opinions, but you can have these beliefs without a lot of negative thoughts, feelings and emotions about someone else just because they don't agree with you. Let them be who they are—and you be who you are. It's really okay. As a matter of fact, I have found it beneficial to simply use such instances as an opportunity to clarify my own thinking on a subject.

The thing to do is to take the "double-thinking" approach that we talked about in Chapter 6 (page 142). Don't stick your head in the sand; you need to see what is happening and handle it. But don't get caught up in it emotionally, and most importantly, don't spend the rest of your day and half the night thinking about it and about how awful the other person is.

Also, it's important to forget about getting even with another person, beating them at their own game or making sure they get what's coming to them (even if you do so only in your own imagination). Such thoughts create powerful fields of negativity, and the worst of it is, they don't necessarily affect the other person, but they do affect *us*. They affect our health, and they affect our world of affairs.

So how do we do this?

Honor and respect the other person as a spiritual being. By doing this, we connect with the Love that is a central force in them and in us.

Easy to do? No, usually not. But this is *absolutely necessary* if we want the best possible relationship with this person as well as our own peace of mind.

The relationship between Cy and Frank illustrates this.

Cy was an outstanding salesman who had just started a new job with a top-flight sales organization. He and I had been working together while he looked for a new job.

Cy was filled with excitement when he reported back on his first day with his new company, except for one thing. When Cy was introduced to the others in the group, one man pointedly ignored him and even turned his head away when the introductions were made. That was Frank, and Frank was the top salesman. Worse yet, both Cy and Frank did a lot of work with auto dealers, which meant their paths were bound to cross when they were working out in the field.

Within a few weeks it was obvious that Frank's rudeness wasn't going to change. Worse, while out in the field, Cy heard a number of things that indicated Frank was actively trying to undermine him. And every morning, Frank pointedly ignored Cy at the sales meeting. His rudeness was apparent to everyone.

Cy was not only a terrific salesman, but he was also very competitive, and he really wanted to come down hard on Frank, so already he had figured out a number of ways to illustrate to the company, as well as potential customers, just what Frank was attempting to do.

2. See the relationship not as it is, but as you want it to be.

I suggested to Cy that he see Frank in a totally different, and loving, way. I said to him that if he could do this, one of three things would happen.

1. *He will change toward you.*
2. *You will leave his world.*
3. *He will leave your world.*

I also assured him that whatever happened would be for the greatest and highest good of all concerned.

Cy decided to take my advice instead of going after Frank as he had imagined. So, every morning Cy got to the sales meeting a bit early and sat outside in his car for a few minutes before going inside. He visualized shaking hands with Frank. He saw the two of them smiling at each other. Some weeks later, he decided to expand his vision and see himself giving Frank a big hug. (Well, the first time Cy saw himself giving Frank a big hug, he also saw himself giving Frank a really hard smack in the middle of his back. But he kept at it until he could imagine it without also giving Frank the hard smack.)

One morning when Cy walked into the sales meeting Frank wasn't there. After the meeting, the company president asked to see Cy in his office. He then told him that Frank had resigned to go into selling commercial real estate. The biggest surprise, though, was that Cy was later asked to take over all of Frank's automotive accounts which, at the time, provided about $35,000 in annual commission income.

But the story doesn't end there. About six months later, it was Christmas and the company had a little party. Unexpectedly, Frank walked in to see all his old friends. He talked for a while with a number of people, and finally, he turned to Cy. After a few minutes of small talk, he blurted out, "I have a confession. I didn't like you at all when I met you." There was an awkward moment before Frank continued, "It really wasn't your fault, and I knew that, but I couldn't seem to help myself." Cy realized then that Frank had deeply resented the competition he had expected would take place between the two of them. Frank continued by saying that for a long time he had wanted to go into commercial real estate, and in taking the new job, he felt that he had finally found his niche. He was very successful, and he loved it. "So, I want to apologize," Frank said. They both smiled and shook hands. Then Frank reached out and put his arms around Cy, and they actually hugged warmly.

One final note. When Cy reflected on this amazing incident later, he realized that Frank was wearing the *same tan suit* that he had imagined him wearing every morning as he sat in his car before the sales meetings visualizing a positive encounter with Frank.

3. Let the relationship find its own true balance. Do not control. Do not manipulate.

Relationships thrive in an environment in which both (or all) parties are respected, honored and allowed to express authentically. Because of this, control and manipulation is always counter-productive. There may appear to be some short-term benefits, but in the long run, a relationship suffers in direct proportion to the degree of control or manipulation by either party.

Especially in close or intimate relationships, you must be able to let go of any need to control or manipulate the other person. Some people may find this quite challenging, but you can only be responsible for your own attitude. If you change it from one of hurt or anger to one of respect and/or love, the relationship will change. At the least, it will change for you, and that will open the door for a spiritual change for the other person, too.

When we are able to let go of negative feelings toward the other person, the relationship is able to find its true level. Yes, we are always in the "right" relationship—one that corresponds to our present consciousness—but *the "true" relationship is the one in which both parties are able to express themselves to their greatest potential.* Sometimes that can be when we are very close in proximity, while at other times, as in the case of Cy and Frank, the true relationship can exist only when the two parties have a lot of distance between them. In some cases, this can be as much as half a world apart. Is this the way it will be forever? No, of course not. But the true relationship can never emerge when both parties are jockeying for position.

When we are focusing negatively on a relationship, or when we are attempting to control or manipulate it, we are pouring attention and energy into *what we don't like about the relationship.*

By focusing our thinking on the relationship as we *want* it to be, we rid ourselves of the glue that holds the relationship in a 'stuck' position, and we let it move to a new level which is for the greatest and highest good of both parties—and that's a Spiritual action guided by an Intelligence greater than our own.

Now, we can't control this action, and we usually can't predict it, either. What we can do is to make it possible and allow it to happen.

However, sometimes the relationship is such that we don't have, or at least don't seem to have, many options. Such was the story with Jayne.

I met Jayne in a meditation/prayer group. She was separated from her husband and had two young sons, ages six and nine, whom she had not seen in over a year. Her husband, a citizen of another country, had taken the boys for a weekend visitation, and they never returned. Weeks later, Jayne's worst fears were confirmed: She learned that her husband and the boys were in her husband's country living with his wealthy and politically-connected parents.

Jayne's family was of moderate means, but by the time I met her they had spent tens of thousands of dollars tracing the boys to the homeland of their father and attempting to establish communication. They had contacted everyone they could think of—friends, investigators, congressmen and consulates. Finally they had exhausted every known legal means, as well as some that were a bit questionable. Jayne's husband was well-shielded, and he was protected from and/or rejected all efforts at communication.

Every day, Jayne spent time doing prayer work and visualization for the return of her sons. She saw herself embracing them. She saw the boys in her own home environment. As she looked out the window and saw the neighbors' children playing outside, she would visualize her sons playing with them.

Her biggest job was letting go of her anger and resentment toward her husband. Instead, she saw herself talking amiably with him. She worked constantly to replace her negative thoughts of him with positive thoughts respecting and honoring his spiritual being.

She also began to focus on the good things in her own life as it was. That was very painful to do initially, but eventually she could focus more and more on positive things in her own world.

Two and a half years went by with no word from her husband. Then, one day out of the blue, her doorbell rang. It was one of her husband's good friends, a man who had previously claimed to have no knowledge of her husband's or the boys' whereabouts. There he was, standing on Jayne's front porch to hand-deliver a letter from her husband. The letter suggested that this man might serve as a liaison in working out an arrangement whereby Jayne would be able to see her children.

It took many weeks, many letters and many tears, but finally an agreement was reached. Initially, both boys spent part of the year with their mother and part of the year with their father. After a few years, however, one of the boys decided he wanted to live permanently with his father and visit his mother only during the summer. The other son decided just the opposite. He wanted to live permanently with his mother and visit his father during vacation times.

Both parents had let go of their angry and hostile feelings enough to let their relationship find its own level. And because of this, as the boys matured, they, too, were able to make their own decisions. Most importantly, the boys had warm, loving feelings toward both parents. They had free and constant contact with them, and most surprising of all, the parents were able to communicate with each other with respect and consideration.

4. When your miracle is to find the "love of your life," keep your own life rich and rewarding.

Every relationship in our personal world has its own special importance, but to most people, the one that we most desire is a deeply fulfilling relationship with a warm, loving and understanding mate. This is the relationship in which we hope to find our greatest fulfillment.

Know that you deserve—truly deserve—warm loving relationships.

Think about that every day, and watch your life change!

If you are looking for your soul mate, you first need to feel worthy of the love you desire, and you need to know that the right and perfect person for you is now moving into your life. You will be drawn to the very activity that leads to the "chance meeting" with Mr./Ms. Wonderful.

Still, the desire for a satisfying and rewarding romantic relationship is one of the deepest we can experience. Because of this, we often feel inadequate if we are not in a relationship. Handling this feeling is frequently our biggest challenge.

Many people go through this searching period feeling, looking and acting pretty much as if their lives are incomplete. They make comparisons between their own lives and what they imagine their friends' lives are like. Or they make comparisons between what their own lives are and what they *could* be *if only* they had a significant other. When they go out to dinner or to a play, rather than focusing on their lovely evening, they move through it with an undercurrent of what they lack rather than an appreciation for what they have.

Do you remember the story about the professor who put a plain sheet of white paper up in front of the class and then made one small black dot on it? When he asked his students what they saw, one after another responded that they saw a black dot. He asked, "All you saw was the black dot? Didn't any of you see the large, beautiful sheet of white paper?"

It is important to remember the spiritual principle that we magnify and increase that to which we give our attention. Our focus needs to be on what we have and not on what we don't have.

Train yourself to appreciate everything in your life that you enjoy, everything that is fulfilling and enriching.

When you do this, you are attracting into your life more people, things and experiences that are enjoyable, fulfilling and enriching.

The most important thing you can do while you "wait" is to "not wait."

Make a commitment to yourself to fully enjoy and appreciate the life you are living, and make your life as rewarding and fulfilled as possible.

Almost every couple has an interesting story about how they met, and we all know many rather incredible stories about "how we got together." One story that illustrates several important points is the story of Marcia and Ted.

Marcia and Ted met when she was nineteen and in college. He was a little older, twenty-three at the time. Marcia was very attracted to Ted. He was everything she wanted in a man, but whenever they were together in the same group, he didn't seem aware of her at all. And then, after a couple of years, Ted became engaged to someone else in their group, married that person and moved to another state.

Although there had never been a "relationship" between them, Marcia loved everything that she knew about Ted. One warm summer evening, a few months after Ted had moved away, Marcia sat alone on the porch outside her home. She sat in the dark for a long time and thought about Ted. She recalled his many wonderful qualities and then thought to herself about how there was no way that it would ever work out for the two of them. Unexpectedly, however, she looked up at the sky and called out in the dark, "If there's any way I can have this man, I love him, and I want him."

As she did this, Marcia felt a great feeling of release. She continued to sit on the porch for a long while, but, somehow, something was now complete for her. Something had changed. After that night, she was able to move on with her life, free of the unfulfilled longing she had previously experienced whenever she thought of Ted.

> She had spoken her word and released it. This also released her to get on with the business of her life.

Subsequently, Marcia graduated from college, met another fine young man and married him. She raised a family of a son and two daughters, and lived a happy and fulfilled life. Occasionally Marcia would run into someone from the old group who made some small mention of Ted, but she didn't see him and they had no contact. Whenever she thought of him, she imagined him living a good life.

It was forty years after the night when Marcia had called out to the stars before she and Ted met again. His wife had died, his children were grown, and he was moving back to the town where he and Marcia had met. She had lived there all these years, and now her husband, too, had died.

Not surprisingly, the feeling was still there—only this time, it was there, too, for Ted. It wasn't long before Marcia and Ted were married, and their life together truly was everything she had ever dreamed it might be. "In fact," Marcia confided to me, "when Ted was younger, he was a bit cocky and arrogant. Now that has all mellowed, and I can hardly believe how lucky I am."

Luck? Hardly!

CHAPTER 9

OBSTACLES OR STEPPINGSTONES?

BY now, you probably have a pretty good idea of how the hidden laws of the Universe work with respect to co-creation and miracles.

As we have discussed throughout this book, there is an Infinite Intelligence, an Absolute Power and an Unconditional Love that is the essence of everything. Whether you call it "Spirit," "God," "Source," or "Higher Power" really doesn't matter. We direct, and It provides. This Intelligence, Power and Love respond to our consciousness, to the sum total of all our thoughts, feelings and emotions. Since we have many differing thoughts and opinions—and even conflicting emotions—on a number of things, Spirit responds to those thoughts and feelings that are the most dominant, or powerful, in our consciousness.

Nothing is lost in consciousness, but there are some very powerful thoughts, feelings and emotions about ourselves and our lives that we often internalize. They remain just below the level of our conscious mind, surfacing briefly but with regularity. We tend to absorb them as part of our being as we continue through life.

When these thoughts and emotions are positive—for example, self-confidence, high self-esteem, feeling secure—they support us in everything we do. They are powerful attractors of good into our world.

However, negative emotions and thought patterns create fields of negativity. They also are strong attractors of negative experiences. I believe: The deepest and most powerful of these negative emotions are guilt (or, when internalized, shame), regret and resentment.

Some people might wonder why anger isn't included in this chapter when we discuss negative emotions. That's because anger falls into one of two basic categories: healthy anger and unhealthy anger. Healthy anger is usually a positive in our lives. It is a feeling that arises when an important need is not met or when we have been intruded upon or violated in some way. Healthy anger can also be a resolve to do better (to lose weight, for example). Essentially, healthy anger moves us to take action to protect ourselves or to change some situation in our lives. Once we take action, the anger dissipates and the experience is productive.

Unhealthy anger, however, is almost always counterproductive. It is a negative emotion that can range from brief, angry outbursts to violent loss of self-control. There is often a sense of injury and a desire for vindication or retribution. This type of anger is, indeed, negative, but it is not a *primary* emotion. It is a *secondary* emotion that stems from a primary emotion (often, resentment). It usually originates from a very early childhood injury (or injuries) and becomes "frozen," a chronic feeling that can become a habitual way of responding to anything that is frustrating us or is not the way we want it to be. The key here is to work with the primary emotion; resolving this will reduce the secondary emotion of anger. You may find help in doing so by reading books on anger and/or the inner child.

In all cases, however:

Anger is a choice. There is always a split second before anger begins to express—a momentary gap between the trigger and the reaction—during which time we can choose differently and/or remove ourselves from the triggering situation.

Thanks in large part to the landmark work of Dr. Hans Selye at the University of Montreal over sixty years ago, the effect of stressful emotions on our health is well-documented today, and widely understood. Selye's work demonstrated that emotional strain and what he called "unpleasant stress" play a very significant role in the development of all types of disease, including high blood pressure, ulcers and some types of mental disorders. (Conversely, Selye also found that pleasant stress contributes to our well-being.)[1]

At the Institute for HeartMath®, they even refer to positive emotions as "assets" and negative emotions as "deficits" to the vital energy that keeps our bodies operating harmoniously and sustains us on a daily basis.

Are you clear on why negative emotions have such wide impact in our lives? Psychotherapist and author Dr. Wayne Dyer puts it like this: He says that they "corrode" our connection to our Source.

I like this analogy, because in one way or another, the negative emotions and thoughts act as filters or blocks to the flow of Infinite Intelligence and Power into our world of affairs. Even worse, as we discussed earlier, they are actually *attractors* of negative experiences.

About this time, you might be wondering if you have to do a complete makeover of yourself in order to see your miracle unfold. No, not at all! You're reading this book because you wanted a *shortcut* to your miracle. The shortcut is knowing what to do, but it also includes knowing what can hinder or delay your miracle.

Powerful negative thoughts, feelings and emotions work against the unfoldment of miracles.

You are the only one who can determine whether or not any of the material in this chapter applies to you. If it does, you'll recognize it and get a new perspective on how to handle these powerful feelings.

Even when you are able to make only small changes in releasing these negatives, you establish new patterns in your thinking.

These patterns have a cumulative effect that profoundly impacts all areas of your life.

Simply by understanding this and by forming the intention to shift your thinking, you begin the process.

By becoming increasingly focused on your intention, you can make small changes, and then larger changes, and then larger still. Finally, one day some months later, you will realize that you have made substantial changes in your thinking. At the same time, you will realize that you are leading a happier, more fulfilled life, and that things in your life seem to be working in harmony together. This is the atmosphere in which miracles take place.

In most cases, when we experience guilt, regret or resentment, we think that the way we feel is the "right" way to feel and we're very certain that anybody else in the same circumstances would feel the same way. Usually, we think it's the *only* way to feel and that we really can't change it. Worse yet, the more we think about it, the more we justify our position and the more susceptible we become to similar pain.

No matter how long these negative thoughts, feelings and emotions have been around, no matter how strong they are, and no matter how well-founded we may feel they are, this is the important principle that applies:

> They are negative patterns of thinking, and we can change them.

The fact is this:

The *incident* does not create the negative emotion. We create it *ourselves* by placing guilt or blame either on ourselves or on someone else.

When we examine such incidents from a different perspective, we can usually find a better way to think, one that allows us to be free of the physical and emotional tightness and tension that accompanies these negatives. When we are able to do this, it also allows us to open more fully to our miracle *even if our negative thought pattern might seem to be totally unrelated to the miracle.*

These negatives are the root cause of some of our key challenges. As we learn to think differently, we open the door to a fuller, richer and more rewarding life. But, possibly of even greater importance for you at this moment, it may even open the door *to your miracle.*

THE DOORWAY TO CHANGE

Imagine that the Creative Power and Intelligence of Spirit are the sunshine outside your window on a bright, clear day. Then think of guilt and resentment as emotions that are like the Venetian blinds on your window. The more powerful your negative emotions, the tighter the blinds and the darker the room. As you release the negative emotions, however, the blinds open and sunlight streams into your room.

In like manner, the Creative Action of Spirit is always present and ready to flow into expression in our world. We open to it, we limit it, we filter it or we block it—all through our thinking. In fact, in many cases:

When we release these powerful negative emotions, that change alone may be all it takes to allow our miracle to appear.

The release changes everything. We feel better. Our thinking clears. Our relationships are more harmonious. And, in many cases, our miracle makes its appearance.

For some people, just reading about a new way to look at things will be enough to help them make big changes in their thinking. For others, it might spark the desire for additional internal work.

It's *your* thinking, and you can change it.

Changing your thinking involves making a shift from one type of habitual thinking to another. We all know that habits, both good and bad, become virtually automatic. We do and think habitual things without having to exert much effort. The downside to this, of course, is that when we want to change our habit(s) and/or our habitual thinking, we go through an unsettling period where we have to focus very carefully and painstakingly on what we're doing in order to make the change(s). But this becomes easier and easier as we go along. And then the day comes when we are able to look back and see what enormous strides we've made! Along with that comes a feeling of inner well-being that is the soil in which our miracles take root and flower.

The first and probably most essential step to reaching your miracle is to become willing to let go of negatives such as guilt, regret and resentment.

Yes, *to become willing*. This is the doorway to the change we are looking for. By becoming willing, we signal to the universe our intention that we want to let go of the things that may have been holding us back. When this happens, we are led to the right people to help us, the right books to read and the right things to do to move us further along our journey.

The release of these powerful negatives transforms them from obstacles into steppingstones on the pathway to a higher consciousness.

This is the pathway not only to the miracle you want right now, but to other miracles in your future as well.

There are three transformational steppingstones. Each of them can be either a major obstacle to miracles... *or* a major steppingstone to a greater miracle-making consciousness. These are:

- Letting go of the past
- Handling guilt
- Handling resentment

In all of these cases:

Forgiveness is the answer.

Let's discuss each one in turn.

LETTING GO OF THE PAST

Trying to move forward in life while holding onto the past is like running a race while looking backwards.

Whenever we hold on to the past, we do so by choice and generally because we believe it was (a) so good it can never be replaced, or (b) so bad it is causing all of our current problems. Although neither of these is essentially true, both become true to the extent that we believe them to be true.

There's nothing wrong with remembering wonderful times of our past. The problem comes when we continue to live there. We probably all know people in their forties and fifties who regularly exhaust their friends with detailed accounts of their college football exploits or references to when they were class president (or when they almost were class president).

I am reminded of the brother of a good friend whose fiancée had broken their engagement a month before their wedding. That happened when he was twenty-five, and when I last knew him he was almost fifty years old, still living at home and refusing to consider new relationships because he was convinced that nothing could compare with the one he had lost.

Any time we stay in the past, we are there by choice.

If we tell ourselves that the wonderful times of the past cannot ever be duplicated in our lives, well, that's probably what's going to happen. Another way of looking at the same circumstances, however, is to know that the wonderful times of the past can prepare us for wonderful times right now as well as wonderful times in the future. There is absolutely no limit on wonderful times, and there is absolutely no limit on wonderful people.

Other times, we hold on to the past because we think we have no choice. We tell ourselves and others, "Well, if this had been *your* experience, you wouldn't be able to let go of it either." Again, this is not true. But, as we have discussed previously, we live in a Universe that responds to our belief, and so it becomes true to the extent we believe it to be true.

In many more cases, people hold on to the past not because it was so good but because it was so bad. For example, a bad childhood can be a continuing excuse for many people in handling the problems they have as adults. A bad marriage can be a continuing excuse for the problems of many other people, and a bad experience at their last job provides grist for the mill for a host of other individuals.

As long as these people continue to relive their bad experiences, they will find themselves handling continuing problems for which they can blame their father, mother, ex-spouse, former boss, etc.

- Simply put, if their problems were due to their bad childhood, then everybody who had an equally bad childhood would experience the same kinds of problems.

- If their problems were due to a bad marriage, then everybody who had an equally bad marriage would experience continuing problems.

- And if their problems were due to a bad job experience, then all the people with a bad job experience would have continuing problems.

But that doesn't happen, and the reason is that many people *choose* to stop blaming their problems on what happened to them when they were children, or what happened to them in their first marriage, or what happened to them at their last job. They learn to let go of their victim stories.

There is a story about two Buddhist monks who were making a three-day journey from one monastery to another. Early on the first morning of their journey, they came to a rather wide but shallow river. On the shore was a very lovely young lady who was attempting to get to the other side. Her skirts were long and full, however, and she feared she would lose her balance and fall.

The younger of the two monks smiled, engaged her in brief conversation, and offered to carry her across. She gratefully accepted, so he picked her up and carried her to the other shore. There he set her down. She thanked him. They all wished each other well and continued their journeys.

That night as they were preparing for sleep, the older monk chided the younger one. "Brother, you committed a sin this morning when you carried that young woman across the river. You were not supposed to touch her."

The younger monk sat still for a moment and then responded, "Yes, my brother, I did carry her across the river. But I put her down on the other side. You have carried her with you all day."

Do you begin to see that when you live in the past you simply compound the pain, reinforce the vividness of the memories, and sacrifice today and tomorrow in the service of yesterday? You also make it much more difficult—or in some cases even impossible—for the miracle to unfold. And you *do* have a choice.

HANDLING GUILT

Feelings of guilt are often excruciatingly painful and make us feel awful about ourselves. Because they are so painful, we tend to push them down and out of our conscious minds as quickly as possible.

Dr. Gerald Jampolsky, well-known psychiatrist and author of *Good-Bye to Guilt,* defines *guilt as* "the feeling of self-condemnation that we experience after we do something that we think is wrong."[2] Whether or not we actually did something wrong is immaterial.

For example, a friend of mine carried enormous buried guilt because she had been told at age six that her naughty behavior had caused her mother's death. You and I can see how abusive and unfair this was to this little girl, but nevertheless, my friend still had to work through her feelings of guilt as an adult. Later on, she also had to release her resentment toward the aunt who had told her this.

In another situation, a man I know carried great guilt because when his company failed, all his employees lost their jobs and their incomes. While it was appropriate for him to feel empathy for the changes in their lives and to assist them if possible, they were all responsible people with talent and abilities, capable of relocating to other good positions. I had to remind him that he had provided wonderful employment and incomes for many people for many years. Every step along the way, he had done the very best he knew how. Now it was time for him to address his own needs.

So, whatever the cause of our guilt, we need to recognize it and confront it before we can release our feelings of guilt.

Most guilt relates to something we have done or not done. We condemn ourselves for whatever it was, and carry that feeling around inside like a big boulder. It weighs us down. It makes us feel beaten down. It destroys our confidence and our self-esteem.

Jampolsky has also found that:

Whenever we experience feelings of guilt, we also anticipate punishment.[3]

Think about it for a moment. Is that really what you want while you are waiting expectantly for your miracle? I don't think so.

Here are two simple approaches to handling guilt. Don't be misled by their simplicity; both are effective. Use one or the other, or both. Repeat them often if necessary. Once you clearly affirm your intention to release your feelings of guilt, the Universe responds. Don't just shove your feelings down; work through them and release them.

For the first approach, literally hundreds of thousands of people in twelve-step programs have freed themselves from the bondage of guilt and moved forward into wonderful new lives by following steps very similar to this four-step process.

1. **Recognize and identify whatever it is you feel guilty about.** In addition to just thinking about it, write down and spell out in detail everything you think you have done that is so terrible. As you do this, you may come to realize that it really wasn't such a big deal after all. (Guilt can sometimes cause the same kind of vague, fearful anxiety that a bad dream has. Writing it down is like turning on the lights and getting rid of the monsters.)

2. **Acknowledge your part in whatever happened that may have hurt someone else.** Try to look back on the situation as objectively and compassionately as possible. Do this without

beating up on yourself and without blaming anyone else.

3. **If there is something you can do to correct the problem or make amends, do it**. Maybe there is a heartfelt apology to be made, or a sincere letter of apology to be written. If the person involved is no longer available (e.g., they may have died or moved away), write the letter anyway, and then burn it. But write the letter with all sincerity.

4. **Release the guilty feeling ("I don't need this any more!") and commit to take *only the lesson* forward with you from now on.** You have recognized it, acknowledged it and made whatever amends are possible. From this point on, resolve to think of the situation only as a learning experience. There is nothing more for you to do. It's complete. It's done. It's over. Let it go.

For some reason, we are less forgiving of ourselves than we ever would be of someone else in similar circumstances. We also set the bar much higher for ourselves than we would for others. Here is a second technique that has proven to be very helpful in such situations.

1. Take two chairs and place them facing each other, a few feet apart. Sit down in one chair

and imagine that a counselor or trusted friend is sitting in the other.

2. Now, tell the imaginary counselor all about what you have done that is causing your guilty feeling. Say as much as you possibly can. Talk about what happened and why it happened. Tell the counselor how you felt then and how you feel now.

3. Now move over to the other chair and be the counselor. Respond to what you have just heard. You will find that there is a part of you that has an amazing compassion and understanding for what took place. Continue the dialog, moving back and forth as necessary. Talk back and forth to the "imaginary you" about whatever it is that "they" have done and try to help them feel better. Almost invariably, you will see things from a completely different perspective. You will feel compassion and understanding totally unlike what you may have been feeling towards yourself. For example, you may see that "This is what kids sometimes do," or that "It wasn't that terrible" or "You did this because at that time you didn't know how to set boundaries, but now you do."

Trust me: Try it. You probably will be able to see the entire situation more objectively. You may also see how hard you've been on yourself.

If you re-envision this dialog whenever feelings of guilt about the situation start to re-emerge, one or more of three things will happen: (1) The guilty feelings will begin to dissipate; (2) you will intuitively become aware of insights that will cause you to see the situation in a more objective light; or (3) something will come to mind as to some corrective action that needs to be taken (and subsequently, the taking of that corrective action will release the guilty feelings).

The answer to handling guilt is self-forgiveness, and this does not take place when we "stuff it down."

These steps may need to be taken again and again until all your guilt is finally gone, but every time you do them, an important part of the work is being done. Think of a sculptor working with a piece of marble. Every tap of his hammer and chisel is necessary to complete the job... and it may require a lot of taps. Do we know how many taps of the hammer Michelangelo had to make before he achieved his David?

HANDLING RESENTMENT

Resentment occurs when we believe we have been wronged or insulted in some way. Someone has done something to us that has wounded us. The injury may be real, or it may be imagined. It may be something recent or it may be from a long time ago. It may be something that happened to us, or it may be something that happened to someone important to us. It all makes no difference, as the effect is the same.

Resentment is usually characterized by a long-standing, powerful negative feeling that simmers just below the surface. But it *does* surface, and regularly. It surfaces when we are reminded of it, and it surfaces in quiet moments when nothing else is taking our attention. In fact, the word *resentment* is derived from the French, *re* meaning "again" and *sentir* meaning "feel." And that's what we do: We feel it again and again. It is "re-sent" and "re-sent."

Unlike feelings of guilt, which we tend to push down and out of our minds as quickly as possible, we tend to clutch onto feelings of resentment in our consciousness, as though reliving our indignation or outrage is somehow going to make things better. We often entertain ourselves with imaginary revenge or one-upmanship.

One of the most successful attorneys I know uses affirmative prayer to release any and all feelings of resentment "anywhere present" in the preparation of all of his cases. When going into court, he visualizes the entire courtroom filled with loving energy that balances and harmonizes every word and action. If there is a jury, he surrounds the jury in particular with thoughts of love and appreciation.

Here are some things to consider about resentment.

- Resentment is the emotional reliving of something unpleasant that happened to us in the past. The more we relive the resentment, the more we keep it going in living color. This keeps us glued to the past.

- By continuing to focus on the feeling of resentment, we not only are filling our minds and bodies with negatives, but we are also laying the groundwork for more negative experiences.

- Even if we somehow "even the score," the victory is usually hollow, and the resentment continues.

- Nothing we can do will change the past. What we can do is to change our perception of what happened.

Possibly, the most important point is this:

**Where there is resentment, there is blame.
When we blame, we have made ourselves a victim.**

As we have already discussed, we are not, or at least we don't *need* to be, victims. When we see ourselves as victims, that's the way the universe responds to us. But when we see ourselves as *victors*—as heroes and heroines—that, too, is the way the universe responds to us.

Regardless of whatever may have happened in the past, the Truth is this:

234

234

You do not need to be a victim.

When you are in control of your thoughts, you are in control of your life.

To be a victor, you must see yourself as a victor.

Some years ago, a friend of mine named Bob was a senior vice president of one of the largest public relations firms in the world. He had been there for twenty-one years and fully expected to work there for the rest of his life.

One day, completely without warning, his boss called him into his office. One of the agency's large clients had filed for bankruptcy, and they owed the agency a lot of money. This money included many man-hours the agency had expended, as well as substantial monies advanced on behalf of the client. So, the agency was out-of-pocket well into six figures. Bob was the supervisor on the account.

It didn't matter that Bob had actually become concerned about the client's financial solvency some months earlier and had taken his concerns to the accounting department, advising them to monitor the account carefully. It didn't matter that he had processed all the out-of-pocket costs immediately, and yet the billing had been tied up for many weeks in the accounting department. (With earlier billing, his company very well might have been paid.) And it also didn't matter that the accounting department was short-handed and running behind in all its work. All that mattered was that the agency was now on the hook for a lot of money and somebody had to be fired.

Within a few minutes, Bob found himself out of a job. *Just like that!* After twenty-one years, he had about half an hour before the close of the business day to clean out all his personal possessions and leave.

For years before this happened, Bob had fantasized that if, for any reason, he left this large agency, he would like to go into business for himself doing the same thing. So, after he had packed up all his personal things and he walked through the doors of the agency for the last time, he said to himself, "Well, now I'm in business for myself."

Some while later, after the shock wore off, Bob realized that if he had left his job by choice, his profit-sharing account would have been fully vested. Because he had been fired, however, he had been divested of certain agency contributions, interest, monies known as "remainders" and such, and it came to a lot of money.

In talking with his lawyer about the papers to form his own agency, Bob asked about this profit-sharing money. After some investigation, his lawyer told Bob that in his opinion, the circumstances of his firing qualified as a "wrongful termination." This would mean that Bob was legally entitled to all the money he would have received had he resigned, plus damages.

The lawyer was so confident of Bob's legal position that he offered to file the necessary lawsuit on a contingency basis. In other words, he would not charge a fee but, instead, would take a percentage of the final award.

That sounded pretty good to Bob, and so the lawsuit was filed.

Bob formed his new company, and it was a very exciting time for him. He was filled with energy and enthusiasm for all he was handling, *except for when he had to talk to his lawyer about the lawsuit against the former agency.*

One night, Bob sat up late thinking. This lawsuit was taking a lot of time and negative energy. He loved the meetings that took place with his lawyer when working on aspects of his new business, but he really disliked the meetings with his lawyer when they went over the materials for the lawsuit. He became aware that after those meetings, he would remain filled with anger and resentment towards his old company for many hours. Also, that his muscles would feel heavy and his mind sluggish, and rather than focusing on the business at hand, he would find himself thinking for long periods of time about the "wrong" that he felt had been done to him.

Bob loved the experience of building his new company, and he knew that now, more than ever, he needed a clear, creative mind and the vital energetic drive he normally experienced. There were probably a couple hundred thousand dollars involved in the lawsuit, but Bob realized his whole future was involved in his new company.

Bob put the two things on a scale, and he made an important decision. Even though there was no cash outlay required on his part in terms of the lawsuit, Bob decided that the emotional cost and energy

*drain was too great. He decided that he was far bet-
ter off putting all his time and energy into the positive path of building his new business. He called his
attorney the next day and told him to withdraw the
lawsuit.*

In that moment, Bob changed from victim to victor.

About six months later, Bob reflected on his decision
and realized that every one of his key clients had followed
him to his new business. He congratulated himself on having made the right decision: The decision to let go of his
resentment and, instead, dedicate his time and energy to
his new undertaking. Now he was making more money
than he had ever before, and he was happier than he had
ever been at the other agency. He realized that being fired
was one of the best things that had ever happened to him.

Bob said this decision provided one of his most valuable life-lessons. He put it this way:

**Sometimes the right decision
is hard to make but easy to live with.**

FORGIVENESS IS THE ANSWER

Every one of us has had things happen in our past
where we felt we were wronged by somebody else. We
may have been lied to; we may have been betrayed; someone may have taken something that belonged to us; someone may have harmed us physically or emotionally (or

both); someone may have broken a promise or let us down in some other important way. Or, one of these things may have happened to somebody we love, somebody we feel responsible for.

Or we may have done something that caused pain or loss to someone else. It may have been something we did unwittingly, something we did intentionally or possibly a situation where we simply should have known better.

Whatever it was, if we are carrying the burden of guilt or resentment, we are expending huge amounts of powerful emotional energy that keep us from moving into the world of miracles. The power of these emotions is like Krazy Glue in terms of keeping us attached to parts of our lives that caused us pain. In all too many cases, we continue to relive that pain—sometimes occasionally, sometimes often—because we don't know what to do about it.

Forgiveness allows us to move out of the past and not bring the painful emotions with us.

Since we magnify and increase that to which we give our attention, our painful experiences are certainly not what we want to re-create in our worlds.

Many people believe that in order to forgive, we have to act and maybe we're even supposed to feel as though what happened to us was okay. Others think we're supposed to pretend "it" never happened. None of this is correct. It did happen, but the simple fact is that as long as we continue to carry and nurture these hurts, the pain of yesterday continues to destroy the beauty of today. Here's how we know this to be so.

The Stanford University Forgiveness Project is one of the largest and most important studies ever conducted on forgiveness. Its co-founder and director is Dr. Fred Luskin, a pioneer in the field of forgiveness training.

Part of the early work of this project dealt with both Catholics and Protestants from Northern Ireland who had lost family members during the many years of fighting and violence. In this project, Luskin demonstrated conclusively that even people with the most devastating of personal losses can learn to forgive—*and when they do, they feel better physically and psychologically.*

Following a one-week forgiveness training program, participants in this project reported less stress, hurt, depression and anger. The hurt they were experiencing when they began the training moved from an 8 or more to less than 4 by the end of the week (on a scale of 1 to 10, with 10 representing the most intense experience of pain). Further, their depression was reduced by 40 percent during this same period. Follow-up measurements taken four and a half months later continued to show the same positive results.[4]

Imagine! People who experienced such personal devastation were able to begin to let go of the pain they had been experiencing, sometimes for years. Surely, if these people can learn to heal the pain of their losses, so can most of us. In fact, these early participants returned to their homeland of Ireland *committed to teaching others how to forgive.*

In *Forgive for Good: A Proven Prescription for Health and Happiness,* Luskin discusses his groundbreaking work and the techniques he uses in his forgiveness training programs. He says there is a simple three-step process that takes place whenever we form a grievance that is interfering with our life.

- We take an offense too personally.
- We blame the other person for how we feel.
- We create a "grievance story."

By "taking an offense too personally," he is not, in any way, diminishing the importance of the event. What he is talking about is this simple fact:

Nothing that happens to us is unique.

In other words, there is virtually nothing that we experience that has not been experienced—in some way or at some time—by a number of other people Knowing that our experience is "shared" helps release some of the pain. For some reason, this simple recognition can aid enormously in allowing us to acknowledge the pain without staying stuck in it.

He also makes this point:

Holding people accountable for their actions is not the same as blaming them for how we feel.

We are the ones who are responsible for how we feel. The upside of this, of course, is that when we are responsible for something, we can change it.

A grievance story, of course, is the story of the painful experience from which we have not healed. As we tell the story, we re-experience the anger or the pain, and we very well may find ourselves telling our story at every opportunity.

People have learned to forgive in many ways, but, first and foremost:

> All of these people began with the *intention* to let go of the pain they were carrying from the experience.

One man told me that as a young lad in school he was betrayed by his best friend. The resentment he experienced was emotionally overwhelming and even resulted in sharp stomach pains. "I finally recognized that I was paying the price all over again every time I thought about it," he told me, "and I decided that the price was too high." After that, any time the incident came to mind, he visualized himself strong-arming it away. He would also say to himself, "I will not let you (the incident) hurt me again." He found out that it worked, and he has used that technique throughout his life for other situations as well. This young man had decided at an early age that life was too short for resentments.

At the other end of the spectrum, a woman told me that it was through her experience as a member of a twelve-step group that she was able to heal from living for years filled with pain and anger due to the emotional abuse she experienced when she was a child. She said when she first tried to "become willing" to forgive, she couldn't do it. So she worked to "become willing to become willing." Finally, after working on this and listening to the stories of fellow twelve-steppers, she finally "became willing to become willing," and from there was able to "become willing." Finally she was able to move to forgiveness. Today, some years later, she is a center of balance and harmony for a stormy and rather dysfunctional family that is slowly but surely learning from her example.

Another man described how he felt unjustly squeezed out of a job, and he couldn't let go of his feelings of rage over the injustice. When he had chest pains that resulted in angioplasty and the insertion of a stent in one of his arteries, he took responsibility for what he had allowed to happen to his body. That was almost twenty years ago. Today, he is a strong, healthy and successful businessman—and he forgives with ease. "The price of not forgiving," he says, "is too great."

Luskin's research also has demonstrated that when we learn to forgive, *we also learn to limit the degree to which we are hurt in the future.*

Forgiveness is the answer—the answer to letting go of resentment as well as letting go of hurts from the past.

And *self*-forgiveness is the answer to letting go of guilt.

- Forgiveness is the simple act of letting go of the painful past so we can move forward.

- It is allowing ourselves to open to the richness and beauty of today rather than the pain of yesterday.

- It is letting go of being a victim.

- It is letting go of our victim story.

- It is recognizing that what happened days, weeks, months or even years ago is less important than what is happening today and tomorrow.

- It is releasing the pent-up energy of the past.

- It is opening to the song of our authentic self.

- It is making way for greater love in our lives at every level.

- It is opening to a greater flow of Infinite Intelligence, Divine Power and Unconditional Love by our own means.

- It is making way for the miracle.

SUMMARY OF YOUR PART
IN THE MIRACLE-MAKING PROCESS

At this point, I want to summarize what we have covered so far regarding your part in the miracle-making process. These points are in the order in which we covered them. If necessary, go back and find the section in the book where a particular point is covered and review it more thoroughly. This review should help you become totally familiar with every point. And even then, you will find that reviewing this summary regularly is very powerful. It will bring a fresh vitality and an increased awareness of the points that are most important for you.

Work to develop and maintain a strong miracle-making attitude. Know that:
- Miracles unfold according to Universal Law.
- Your miracle is possible.
- Your miracle is never too big.
- You play a major role.
- You deserve miracles in your life.

Next, get rid of the negatives and make way for the miracle. Let go of:
- Complaining
- Blaming
- Self-criticism
- Criticism of others

- The "coulda," "shoulda," "woulda" syndrome
- Envy

These things apply to all miracles:
- Be very clear. (Focus on "What," not "How" or "When.")
- Expect the best.
- Let go of fear (especially the fear that it won't happen).
- Open your mind to all possibilities.
- See yourself as you want to be.
- Keep the power. Don't talk about it.
- Do what needs to be done by you.
- Pray. Pray often.

If your miracle is in the area of Health, remember:
- Health is our natural state.
- See yourself healthy.
- The Infinite Healing Power operates by Law and not by caprice.

If your miracle is in the area of Success, remember:
- Place no blame. You can only change that for which you are responsible.
- Make sure your attitude is positive. Love what you do—or at least, enjoy it!
- Even our bodies respond to our desire to express creatively and successfully.

If your miracle is in the area of Prosperity, remember:
- Know that you are worthy and deserving.
- There is One Source, but many channels. The Source is always providing for us.
- Make sure your intentions are pure.

If your miracle is in the area of Relationships, remember:

- As we change consciousness, the relationship will change.
- See the relationship not as it is, but as you want it to be.
- Let the relationship find its own true balance. Do not control or manipulate.

Work with Forgiveness to move through the blocks of Guilt, Fear, Resentment and Regret.

Focus on the feeling of the outcome rather than how long it is taking.

Love yourself. Appreciate yourself. Be gentle with yourself.

CHAPTER 10

IN THE FULLNESS OF TIME, OR WHY IS IT TAKING SO LONG?

"**IS** it happening? Is it going to happen? If it's going to happen, when is it going to happen? Where is it? I want it NOW! RIGHT NOW!!"

The more important the miracle,
the more anxious the wait.

This is a vital and constructive time in the miracle-making process. One of the biggest fears we can have is that our prayers won't be answered. Fear, remember, is the opposite of faith. So it's important to handle this fear, but how do we do this?

Focus on the outcome and the feeling of the outcome rather than on how long it is taking.

As we've discussed, sometimes the miracle can happen very quickly, as in the case of Larry when his aneurysm simply disappeared, or Sheldon when his cancer went into permanent remission. Or it can unfold *somewhat* quickly, as it did with Tom and the $40,000 he needed for his business. In other cases—in *many* cases, and maybe even *most* cases—it takes more time.

Whatever length of time it takes, we need to continue to remind ourselves:

It is *really* happening.

When we do this, are we kidding ourselves about the reality of it all? No, not at all. What this means is that *it is happening,* but it's happening in ways of which we are unaware. Remember that we are working with the *hidden* laws of the Universe, where things move from the invisible into the visible. So, your miracle *is* moving into expression in your life, but not yet in ways that you can see and understand.

See it as an "incubation" period
rather than a "waiting" period.

Think for a moment about how a seed grows. After the seed is planted, it germinates. Then, it begins an incubation period while it develops and grows, but for a long time, we don't see any sign of that growth. At last, we see something—little spots of green that soon begin to show as emerging leaves, and, finally, the plant takes form and grows to maturity. In the beginning there's a lot going on, but we don't see it happening. That's what it's like with miracles, too.

There are a couple of other things that are similar in terms of the growth of the plant and the unfoldment of the miracle. The seed needs to be planted in fertile soil, and:

The fertile soil for the miracle, of course, is Spiritual soil, which contains all the elements necessary for the perfect expression of your miracle.

Then, in order for the seed to germinate and grow, it has to have the right nourishment and the proper environment. Again, that's true with miracles. But here *we* are the ones who are responsible for providing the nourishment as well as the environment that make it possible for the miracle to express.

Your thinking provides the nourishment, and your emotional expectancy provides the environment for your miracle.

Spiritual Law works in divine order. The Greeks have a wonderful word for this: kyros, which translates, roughly, as "in the fullness of time," or "when everything is ready for the appearance of the good." Think about what this means. Our miracle is unfolding in Divine Order and will unfold when it's *right* for it to unfold, and not before. It means it will unfold when all things are in order for the miracle. When we truly understand this, we are able to get on with our lives and await our miracle with joyous expectancy.

After all, when you're waiting for a seed to sprout or an egg to hatch, you don't wonder whether it's going to happen or not. You don't pull the ear of corn to make it grow faster, and you don't poke a hole in the eggshell to see what's happening. You wait *patiently and expectantly*, knowing that it is happening, that the process is at work and that the results will show themselves at the right time.

> As long as you are focused on what you want rather than on what you do not want, your miracle is on its way.

At the end of Chapter 9, I have provided a brief checklist of your part in the miracle-making process. One of the most helpful and powerful things you can do is to review it often because this is how you nourish your miracle and provide an inviting environment.

Essentially, your part in the process is a change in consciousness, and that requires consistent, dedicated effort. The more familiar you are with your part in the process, the quicker and more consistently you will be able to catch yourself when any "old thinking" starts to take over. As you do this, you align your thoughts more and more with the miracle-making Power and Intelligence of Spirit and the hidden laws of the Universe.

You are in charge of your thinking, and your thinking needs to be focused on and correspond to what you want. At first, you may find that you need to correct your thinking many times during the day (and night.) Like anything else, however, this becomes easier and more habitual as time goes on.

This is a work-in-progress, just as our lives are a work-in-progress. When we want a miracle in our lives, it pays big dividends to give extra attention to cleaning up our thinking. One of the really nice things about doing this is that the dividends continue on and on after we've formed new thought patterns.

We've talked about this before, but it's important not to berate yourself for any slips in your thinking. Remind yourself that you are simply correcting some habitual thinking that no longer serves you well (for example, decide and affirm, "I don't need this any more!"). Besides, you get an added bonus as you make these changes in your thought patterns: You will find yourself more relaxed, more energetic and more in harmony with everything in your world.

You may be saying to yourself, "Forget that stuff. I just want my miracle!" Don't worry, you'll get that, too.

Once you have clarified your desire either by putting it in written form or in prayer (preferably, both), the seed has been planted, and the miracle is now in the incubation process.

It's important to eliminate, as much as possible, any uncertainty or fear that your miracle might not take place. These are limiting thoughts and they tend to hinder the unfoldment of the miracle. Remember, when you have at least 51 percent faith, you're on the right side of the continuum from fear to faith.

Sometimes it's helpful to be aware of the types of things that might be taking place during the incubation process. You can see how essential they are in the unfoldment of the miracle. Let's look at them closely.

YOUR FEELINGS ABOUT YOUR MIRACLE

When you think about the reality of your miracle as having actually taken place, are all of your feelings positive? For example, if you are praying for your "soul mate," do you feel thoroughly comfortable about the idea of being in a committed relationship? Or if you have somebody special in mind, are there some things about that person that you want to change first?

If your miracle is to own the right and perfect home, do you get uptight when you think of the mortgage payments or the continuing maintenance and upkeep? Are you concerned about future home values in that particular neighborhood or, maybe, a long commute to work?

If the wonderful new job offer happens to be in a part of the country you don't really want to live in, are you secretly hoping you'll be able to subsequently transfer to wherever it is that you *really* want to live?

In other words, is there a downside to your miracle? If so, don't make light of it, and don't push it aside.

**Confront any possible downside
and clarify your thinking.**

Your emotional expectancy provides the environment for the miracle, and if your emotional expectancy is divided—if you are up one minute and down the next—you're sending mixed messages about your miracle. Obviously, this will have a profound effect on what happens in your life.

Several years ago, I worked with a very lovely young lady named Sylvia who had been diagnosed with a "terminal" heart condition. She had been told by every doctor who saw her that the only thing that could save her was a heart transplant but every doctor she saw also told her that for other medical reasons she was not a candidate for a transplant.

For the longest time, nothing seemed to be happening in our work together. Finally, I said to her, "If you were vibrantly healthy today, what would be the worst thing that might happen because you had regained your health?" Sylvia's answer was a complete surprise. "My ex-husband wouldn't have to pay any more child support, and I don't know how I could take care of myself and my two children financially."

Of course! How could she possibly allow herself to be restored to health if it meant she would have no income?

We immediately began to focus our work on her ability to support herself and her children. Sylvia was very creative and had a great deal of talent and ability. Because of her family demands, however, it had been some years since her employment was anything other than sporadic. We discussed the many business opportunities open to her and how she might pursue them.

Slowly but surely, Sylvia's focus changed from one of financial fear to one of confidence about her future. Instead of silently worrying about how she would support herself, this creative and talented woman became excited about the many opportunities that would be open to her once she regained her health. Finally, she began to see herself healthy and financially successful.

By the following year Sylvia's physical condition had improved and she was accepted for a heart transplant.

Each of us has a whole complexity of desires and needs. Conflicting desires are not uncommon, and what they often indicate is that something in our consciousness is not in harmony with what we want. These inharmonious ideas and feelings will always reveal themselves if we are open to them. Be grateful when they do, because until we address them directly, they are lodged in our subjective mind and can delay the arrival of our miracle. We need to allow them to surface so we can face them, handle them, and, in most cases, dispense with them.

Whenever you think about your miracle, if you get any feelings of discomfort *at all,* you need to stop and examine those feelings. Address them. Think them through. Write them down. Work them out.

If you can't get comfortable with *all* the feelings related to your miracle, you may want to rethink whatever it is that you desire. Be very clear on which is more important to you—your miracle or your concerns about what else might come along with your miracle—and why.

The more harmonious all your thoughts and emotions are with your miracle, the more Unlimited Power you are giving to its unfoldment.

And unless all your thoughts about your miracle are harmonious, not only are you inviting delay, but you are inviting an out-of-sync result into your life.

SOMETIMES, THINGS EVEN APPEAR TO GET WORSE

Paradoxically, it's not uncommon for a positive change in our lives to be preceded by a chaotic period in which a number of unsettling things take place. This "getting worse" is often part of things getting better.

In some cases, "getting worse" may simply be the residue of our old consciousness. More often, however, when we have begun the mental and emotional process that allows a miracle to move into our lives, we experience a clearing in consciousness. This clearing in consciousness often results in the shifting around of many things and many patterns in our lives.

This ties in with what is known in quantum physics as _chaos theory_. In 1977 a Belgian chemist named Ilya Prigogine won the Nobel Prize for recognizing that at the quantum level, disorder can be the source of a new order. In other words, a process takes place in which a quantum system reorganizes at a higher level. In order for this to happen, however, there is a breaking down in the existing system. This dissipation is essential to allow the system to reorganize and restructure. Although the process appears to be chaotic, it is completely orderly, and the system actually self-organizes to a higher level of complexity.

The sudden appearance of order out of chaos is the rule rather than the exception. If you think back over your own life, you will probably find instances where this has occurred.

This is another example of things we have learned from the quantum level: "What is true at one level is true at all levels."

No matter what it looks like, beneath any chaotic appearance lies order and harmony.

This is an essential Truth of the creative action of Spirit, so remember the importance of chaos theory when you are praying for a miracle and things seem to be going out of control.

It's very easy to become discouraged, angry or upset, and to think and speak with great emotion during times of chaos. Whenever you do this, of course, you are sending powerful but negative messages to the Universal Power and Intelligence that is always responding to you.

No matter what is happening, stay focused on your miracle and not on unfavorable circumstances. Remind yourself, again and again if necessary:

Things are working *for* you, not *against* you.

One of the inherent qualities of Spirit is harmony. Because of this, there is an essence of harmony in every person, in every relationship and in every situation. Nothing is exempt from this Spiritual truth.

**Despite any apparent chaos,
the essence of everything is harmony.**

Regardless of what may be happening in your life, this says it all as far as how and when your miracle will appear:

**You provide the consciousness.
Spirit makes it happen and finds the perfect way.**

YOU MAY NOT BE READY
FOR THE THING YOU WANT

I can almost hear you saying, "What do you mean 'not ready for the thing I want?' I'm ready, and I'm ready right now!'" Of course you feel that way. It's important for you to feel that way! But usually our lives change incrementally because our consciousness changes incrementally. It's only when we are able to look back that we can see how our readiness grew over time, slowly but surely. That's part of what happens with continued prayer.

And I'm sure that all of us have seen situations where an enormous amount of good (usually financial) moves into someone's life rather suddenly, and their life goes into a tailspin because they weren't ready to handle it.

As you continue to wait expectantly for your miracle, you are becoming more and more prepared for it at deeper levels.

And, as the miracle unfolds, there is still another side to "being ready," and it applies to the circumstances of the miracle itself. The story of two young men in advertising illustrates this.

Don and Ed were account executives at a retail advertising agency. Many of the clients they serviced were small businesses, and comprised accounts they had prospected and developed themselves. The two men had coffee frequently, exchanging ideas and even teaming up together in servicing larger accounts that one or the other developed. Both men were successful and, within a short period of time, became the two top men in the agency.

There was a big problem, however. The agency they worked for had some unethical practices that Don and Ed were not aware of until they had been with the agency for several years.

Added to this, some of their clients had begun complaining about the way they were being treated by the agency. There was rudeness on the telephone, errors in billing and, despite Don and Ed's best efforts, some sloppy production in the advertising campaigns.

Over a period of time, many of their long-time clients began suggesting that Don and Ed start their own agency.

After a while, they began to think this might be the best thing to do for their clients as well as themselves.

There was one big obstacle, however. All of the account executives in the agency had been required to sign employment agreements that had a very stringent non-compete clause. If they left the agency, Don and Ed were restricted in two areas: (1) they couldn't form a new agency within fifty miles of the city of Chicago, and (2) they couldn't work with any of their clients for a minimum of two years.

They talked to an attorney who researched the situation and told them the restrictions were probably far too stringent to be enforced. Recent court rulings held that in most cases geographic restrictions were invalid, and, with respect to working with agency clients, the maximum time restriction upheld by the courts was usually six months.

The attorney suggested that Don and Ed start their agency, and he offered to attempt to negotiate them out of their employment contracts. If that failed, he suggested that one approach would be to simply proceed unless and until they were sued by their former agency. In that case, they could go to court with four or five clients and get a court ruling on the validity of the employment agreement.

So that was what they did. They gave thirty days' notice to their employer, but they were asked by the agency president to leave immediately. Later, the attempt to negotiate their employment contracts failed, so they followed up with a more-than-fair offer to buy their old company with a projected payout over the next ten years. This offer, too, was turned down.

Don and Ed then moved ahead with their plans to form a new business, but within the first ninety days, they found themselves as defendants in a three-count lawsuit that totaled hundreds of thousands of dollars.

The day of the first hearing was one both Don and Ed said they would never forget. Both men had invested heavily in their new company; and if the judge ruled against them, they were out of business before they even began—with no visible means of starting over again.

Four of their clients were going into court with them, and one of them had a very large campaign that was ready to start. The company's grand opening was scheduled to start that very weekend and run for thirty days. The work was all done. The print ads would begin running the next day, and the broadcast commercials had been cut and were already at eighteen radio and television stations, *scheduled to start running at three p.m. that very day.*

Ed said later that he was so nervous his mind simply wouldn't work. He tried to do an affirmative prayer that morning and nothing would come to him. He could hardly think. Still, he wanted a strong affirmation and tried to search his mind for something powerful. The words that came to his mind—and the only words that came to his mind—were these:

There is one Life. That Life is God.
That Life is my life right now.

Ed silently repeated these words to himself over and over and over again.

The judge questioned the four clients individually, asking only three questions. He asked each man his name, the name of his company, and whether Don or Ed had ever handled the advertising for that company. Each of the first three men owned businesses that had advertised with Don or Ed, and the judge ruled that they had to wait six months to advertise through the men's new agency.

The fourth man was the client whose campaign was scheduled to start that same day. He owned a business that *had* advertised with Don and Ed, but he was there representing a new business, one that had never advertised with them before. The judge's decision could have gone either way.

The judge ruled that the business and not the individual was the client; therefore, Don and Ed could handle the new company. Both Don and Ed went weak with relief.

There was one other decision that was especially important. The judge ruled that a six-month restriction was reasonable when it came to all other clients. But as it happened, early in the hearing the former agency had intentionally misrepresented the date of Don and Ed's termination in an attempt to make it appear that they had violated the employment agreement in yet another area. In calculating the six-month period, the judge went back to his notes and used the misrepresented date in determining the start of the six months.

This misrepresentation by the former agency actually cut thirty days off Don and Ed's waiting period so they only had to wait another three months (from the date of the ruling) before they could work with their clients.

This was another important ruling because the largest of their clients was a seasonal advertiser whose campaign had to begin *exactly five months* from the date on which Don and Ed had given notice. If Don and Ed's former company had not attempted to make Don and Ed look bad (with the result being that the judge had miscalculated the restriction date), the major client would have had no choice but to work with someone else in order to meet its advertising needs for that season.

The story of Don and Ed illustrates the enormous power of faith even in the midst of overwhelmingly fearful circumstances. It is also a good illustration of what can happen when you keep your intentions pure. Don and Ed made every effort to be scrupulously fair and above-board in everything they did, and the other agency intentionally misrepresented them to the judge to "paint them black." Later, that misrepresentation became the very thing that cost that agency the largest of their clients.

In the months following the court's decision, Don and Ed had mixed feelings. They knew they had much to be grateful for. The lawsuit had been dismissed and everything regarding the clients was clarified. They were also grateful to have their wonderful new client who was providing work for their staff as well as much-needed revenue to help support the business as it got on its feet.

Despite all this, they couldn't help but shake their heads sometimes and wish they had been allowed to work with all of their clients right away. Whenever this happened, however, they would remind themselves, "This is all for the best whether or not we are able to see it." Meanwhile, they went about doing the endless myriad of business and administrative matters involved in starting a new business. They also developed a wonderful campaign for their new client, and went out and developed other new business. The three months passed, and it wasn't long before their other clients came aboard.

One day, about a year after they had started their business, Don and Ed were reviewing their first year. As they looked back, they realized for the first time that if they had been allowed to work with all their clients when they first started, they *never could have serviced the business*. They didn't have the staff, the systems or sufficient experience in running a company. In all likelihood, they might well have lost some of their good clients. The delay that initially had made them unhappy was *the very thing* that gave them the time they needed to establish their shop as a sound, solid and responsible agency.

Don and Ed laughed as they looked back and realized that a year earlier if anyone had asked them if they were ready to handle all the business, they would have chorused, "We're ready! Of *course* we're ready!" At the time they had no idea they were not completely prepared for the thing they wanted. Only in retrospect could they see how perfect the timing of their miracle had been.

**Sometimes the stage isn't
quite ready yet for your miracle.**

The Intelligence guiding and directing your miracle is present everywhere and is operating for the greatest and highest good of everybody. Trust It.

THE THING YOU WANT MAY NOT BE READY FOR YOU

It often happens that while we are waiting for our miracle to unfold, in our anxiousness we may attempt to force the first thing that comes along and try to make that our perfect answer. In other words, while we're waiting for our miracle to unfold, we may be tempted to "get off the train before we get to our stop." This can easily happen when we're looking for a soul mate, a new job, a new house or a financial solution.

When the right thing appears, it's a wonderful experience for everybody to be able to look back and see how miraculously (and naturally) it unfolded.

We don't need to force or manipulate miracles. They unfold without gut-wrenching effort or manipulation.

Remember Virginia and Robin from Chapter 4? The healing of Robin's aneurysm was one of the miracles this family experienced, and the story of their new home is another. It illustrates how important it is not to get side-tracked by circumstances that seem negative but, rather, to keep focused on what you want.

At the time of Robin's accident, her parents and all five children were living in an 1,800 square foot home. It was very small. There were three levels, three bedrooms and one and a half baths. After Robin's accident, she had to be carried up and down from the lower level, where she slept, to the first-floor living level.

One day Virginia called me, very excited. Their attorney had negotiated a settlement with the insurance company, and although all the details weren't worked out, they were getting a substantial amount of money toward the purchase of a new home. Virginia even had found a lovely house already. The whole family had seen it, and they were excited beyond words over the prospect of moving into this larger home. It had 2,800 square feet, five bedrooms and three baths. Best of all, it was a ranch; everything was on one level. The family wouldn't have to carry Robin up and down the stairs any more. It was a dream come true for everybody.

Virginia was thrilled over the prospect of the new home, but she had misgivings about the financial pressure of the taxes, the maintenance and all the other expenses that go with home ownership. In order to finance the new home, they would have to sell their existing home for top dollar—and right away, too. "It's a real stretch for us," she told me, "and I don't want my family to have to live on a diet of macaroni and cheese at nineteen cents a box." We talked further, and Virginia realized that the moving expenses would add to the financial pressure as well.

We finished our discussion with an affirmative prayer, and I assured Virginia that if this home was the right and perfect place for them nothing could stand in the way of their offer being accepted and closing without a problem. The money they needed would be there, and all the apparent obstacles would be worked out perfectly.

I assured her further that if, for any reason, this deal fell through, it was only because there was something better waiting for them.

Sometimes one thing doesn't happen because something better is waiting to happen.

Virginia and Ken asked their attorney to see if the insurance company would also pay for their moving expenses. They wouldn't. This led to some strained feelings between Virginia, her husband Ken and the attorney. And although they were only a few thousand dollars apart on the offer, the sellers wouldn't come down, and the insurance company wouldn't come up— "not another penny." Virginia and Ken were already stretching to the limit, and they simply couldn't swing it. The deal fell through. Everyone in the family was disappointed. And owning a larger home was becoming more important day by day: The family had learned that a new baby was on the way.

The day after the deal fell through, Virginia was telling one of her friends about this latest turn of events and how upset their lawyer was with them for not being able to come up with additional monies. The friend suggested, "Why don't you get another lawyer? You're having a lot of problems with this one." In view of the hard feelings over the offer that fell through, this last suggestion sounded right to both Virginia and Ken, and so that was what they did.

They got another lawyer and began house-hunting all over again. Virginia said she knew there was something better waiting for them, and she could hardly wait to find it.

It took another four months, and a new lawyer, but three things happened. First, a really magnificent home came on the market. It was in one of the most desirable sections of the city. Rather than 2,800 square feet, *it had 6,000 square feet* of floor space. It had six huge bedrooms and five baths, including a Jacuzzi in the first-floor bedroom suite that would be Robin's. It had a state-of-the-art kitchen, a formal dining room, an office, huge closets and *three* laundry rooms. It had a large indoor swimming pool and a one-half basketball court inside. And if that wasn't enough, it was wheelchair accessible!

Second, they made a very fair offer that was quickly accepted by the sellers. No haggling.

This new home, obviously, was far more expensive than the one on which they had bid. Where had the necessary money come from?

The family's new attorney had renegotiated with the insurance company, and the new settlement was far more substantial. It not only paid *in full* for the home but it covered their moving expenses. This meant that the equity from Virginia and Ken's former home would become their own money to use for other things.

Plus, all this took place just a few weeks before the new baby was born.

Often with miracles, we feel a certain time element is an absolute "must." When we arbitrarily establish a time pressure, however, we are interfering with an agenda that is far larger than anything we can possibly foresee or understand at the present moment. This larger agenda may involve circumstances, things or people of which we may be completely unaware and over which we have no control.

When we allow the miracle to unfold "in the fullness of time," it will unfold with the greatest ease and for the greatest and highest good of all concerned. But, if we attempt to short-circuit the process through pushing or manipulation, we are apt to end up with a far-less-desirable result.

Virginia and Ken's disappointing experience with the offer on the first house was the very thing that catapulted them to a new lawyer, to a settlement which was many times greater than before, and to a larger, more beautiful home which met many more of the needs of their family members—all without financial stress. Not having their offer accepted on the first house was the best thing that could have happened to them.

All things were working in their favor. All things are working in *your* favor, too.

STAY FOCUSED ON WHAT YOU WANT

Sometimes, we can't figure out how what we want can possibly happen. We think nothing will work. Every time we think of a possible answer, there is an even better reason why it can't work that way.

That's what Margaret was going through with respect to her mother. Margaret is the oldest of seven sisters. She was born in Ireland and is the only member of her family living in this country. Although she has lived here for a number of years, she has remained close to her family. She calls her mother daily (briefly, but daily), and returns to Ireland to visit at least twice a year.

Her mother was in her eighties and had been living alone in the family home for many years. However, she had become progressively less able to care for herself. She has to use a walker, and her doctor recommended that she go into a nursing home. Aside from the fact that it was prohibitively expensive, Margaret's mother absolutely didn't want to move anywhere else, and she didn't trust anyone to come in and take care of her. Neither did Margaret nor her sisters.

I suggested to Margaret that every time she thought of her mother, she should visualize her happy, healthy, and well cared for. Then, we did an affirmative prayer together.

That was a little over a year ago. Shortly thereafter Margaret's sisters agreed that they would take turns caring for their mother for extended periods of time. One of them took a leave of absence from her job and spent the last year caring for her mother. It was not good for either of them. They were both unhappy, and before the year was up, it was apparent to everybody that having the sisters rotate care of their mother was not going to work.

During this year, however, Margaret continued daily meditation in which she visualized her mother happy, healthy and well cared for. Despite her daily phone calls home, she did not get caught up in the emotion of her sisters. She kept reminding herself that the opposite end of the problem is the perfect solution. When she went to visit, she stayed out of any emotionalism in their discussions of how to handle their mother's increasing infirmity. She also kept reminding herself that it was not up to her to figure out "how." That was the job of Spirit. Her job was to maintain the vision of "what"—to focus on the end result.

Margaret called me several months ago and said, "What has happened is absolutely unbelievable. This woman simply appeared out of nowhere to take care of my mother, and my mother loves her." Apparently, during the past year, a local woman had helped out for a few hours one day when the caretaking sister was unavailable. That was the only contact, just a few hours. Margaret's mother had liked her.

For some unknown reason, all of the mother's resistance to having someone else care for her melted away. She herself called the woman to ask if she would consider long-term care. After some discussion and some thinking, she and the woman had reached an agreement.

Margaret is simply elated over the changing circumstances and can hardly believe all that has happened in the past few months. This woman really loves caring for Margaret's mother and shows it in many ways, including fresh flowers to brighten the day—and even a home-made birthday cake. Margaret says her mother is truly thriving and has a youthful glow that Margaret hasn't seen for years. Not only is her mother happier and healthier, so are all the sisters. So is Margaret.

Margaret ended our conversation by saying, "If anyone had told me a year ago that something like this was possible, I would have thought they were crazy. But no matter what was happening—or rather wasn't happening—I kept seeing my mother happy, healthy, and well cared for."

Margaret's story also illustrates that the incubation period for a miracle is really a very special period of time. It is an opportunity for you to continue to hold fast to your vision of the end result, knowing your miracle is unfolding perfectly "in the fullness of time." It is also a wonderful opportunity for your personal growth in both faith and consciousness.

Once you experience this in your own life, you will know what I mean, and you will not forget it.

CHAPTER 11

KEEP THE MIRACLES COMING

MOHINI was a white tiger at the Washington, D.C. National Zoo. Every day, she paced back and forth in her twelve-by-twelve-foot cage, a routine that was broken only by her regular feedings, her afternoon naps and her nightly sleep. Finally, after many years, the zoo created a beautiful new environment for her, one much like what her natural habitat would have been in the wild. The new area covered several acres, and it had many wonderful trees and hills and ponds.

The staff watched excitedly when Mohini was finally released to her beautiful new home. They could hardly wait to vicariously share her exuberance at her new-found freedom. Instead, they were puzzled and watched in disbelief as she slunk down and quickly sought refuge in a far corner of her new habitat. There she stayed for the remainder of her life, pacing back and forth in a twelve-by-twelve-foot area. Her routine was broken only by her regular feedings, her afternoon naps and her nightly sleep.[1]

Having read this far, you, like Mohini, have moved into a beautiful new environment in your own world—one that allows you to move freely and expressively in your life, one that allows you to enjoy richness and fullness in your life beyond anything you have previously enjoyed. Are you going to take advantage of it?

The area into which you have now moved is unlimited.

There is untold talent and ability within you right now waiting for expression, and there are limitless opportunities for the expression of this talent. You now recognize that you are a co-creator of your own life through your consciousness, and you now know that there is an invisible world of endless possibilities ready and waiting to support all of your dreams—to provide all your miracles.

One of the wonderful things about continuing to support the unfoldment of the miracle for which you bought this book is that you are also opening the door to a continuing flow of miracles in your life. As you open your consciousness to welcome this first miracle, you are actually changing the direction of your life in all areas. You are laying the groundwork for Spirit to continue to work miraculously in your world. The maintenance of this groundwork is simply the continued clear thinking and emotional expectancy that makes miracles.

In order to fully explore and enjoy this new and unlimited area into which you have now moved, it is important that you continue to support the changes you have been making in your thinking and the new way in which you see yourself.

This puts you into the flow of Infinite Good. As you begin moving in this direction, it becomes easier and easier to lead a life of miracles.

Does this mean you won't have problems and challenges, detours and disappointments in your life? No, of course not. What it does mean, however, is that, more and more, you will be in charge of your life. You will begin to see your problems, challenges and disappointments from a different perspective, and you will be able to respond to and handle them in new and affirmative ways that are life-enhancing rather than self-defeating. You will find yourself growing through your problems rather than being defeated or discouraged by them. They, too, will become steppingstones rather than obstacles.

To rephrase what we discussed in the last chapter:

Our thinking provides the nourishment, and our emotional expectancy provides the environment for all our miracles.

In order to do this most effectively, it is important to develop a personal spiritual practice, one that you follow regularly.

Do you *have* to do this? Well, no, but if you simply read this book and go on about "business as usual," you will probably experience what I call the "parachute effect." This means that just as a parachute sails slowly back down to earth, we tend to do the same thing. In other words, without continued reinforcement of our increased spiritual awareness, we slowly shift back to our old manner of thinking. When we do this, it means that, like Mohini, we are on our way back to our very own twelve-by-twelve-foot space.

A friend of mine likens her own spiritual practice to the greenhouse in which her daughter grows beautiful and exotic orchids in an otherwise hostile climate. The orchids (which feed from the air, by the way, *not* the soil) are maintained in a balanced environment of moisture, light and temperature. My friend points out that her spiritual practice provides the nourishment, environment and spiritual Light that makes miracles.

If the idea of a personal spiritual practice is new to you, it might be a little intimidating. Also, you might feel, initially, that you really don't have the time. Try it for six weeks—oops! Correction! Don't *try*! Decide what you want to do, and *DO* it for six weeks. This is usually enough time to form a new habit.

More importantly, when it comes to a spiritual practice, I think you will find something within urging you to continue by the end of six weeks. That something is Spirit Itself within you yearning for the regular communication you will have established.

Regularity and consistency are the most important elements of any personal spiritual practice.

Most people who follow a personal spiritual practice spend at least a few minutes every day reading some book or magazine that is supportive of their spiritual beliefs. This is a wonderful time to expand your knowledge, deepen your awareness and broaden your understanding.

Journaling has also become increasingly recognized as a sound spiritual practice. This is not like writing in a diary. Entries in a diary are usually chronological and generally relate to daily events, whereas journaling is a written expression of internal thoughts and feelings that may or may not be triggered by daily activities. Journal entries are generally a written stream-of-consciousness that deals more with feelings than with events. It's a process that allows for self-expression and self-understanding at a progressively deepening level. Journaling also has been proven to be amazingly beneficial in physical healing.[2]

There are many types of spiritual practice for us to choose from, and many ways to do them. The important thing is to *do* them. Here are four that I use regularly myself, and I offer them for your consideration—or as a possible starting place.

- Meditation
- Affirmative prayer
- Visualization
- Affirmations

MEDITATION

It's very helpful to precede your prayer time with a period of meditation. This is a tremendously important spiritual practice because it puts us in touch with the Truth of our being, Spirit. Earlier I mentioned that some of the principles of miracles have been esoterically known for untold centuries. This is what I was referencing: The mystical knowledge, long-held, that we are one with the One that created us.

As we expand the recognition of our own spirituality, there is a reciprocal expansion in our lives by the Infinite Power of the Universe. Every time we recognize more about our own spiritual potential, Spirit reciprocates by providing more. This not only means that we express more of our own spiritual qualities in our daily lives, it also means that Spirit increasingly is at work balancing, harmonizing, providing, guiding and directing us as we move through life.

And the wonderful part of it is that we begin to *really know* this is so. We *feel* it on the inside and we *experience* it on the outside.

**As we get a greater idea of ourselves,
greater things happen in our lives.**

Many wonderful things happen in meditation. Some are physical, and some are spiritual. The most noted pioneer in the area of physical benefits was Herbert Benson, M.D., whose research work during the 1960's revealed that daily meditation has a very positive effect in lowering blood pressure and pulse rates of heart patients.[3] Since then, numerous other studies have shown that those who meditate also experience reduced stress and strain, are less irritable, go through the day with greater clarity, make better decisions and enjoy a greater sense of well-being.

To summarize why this is so:

**When we meditate, we are
totally immersed in and by the Infinite.**

In the outer world, we have become accustomed to the idea that in order to "be" something, we first have to "do" something. So the process we generally think of for happiness and success is "Do, Have, Be." However, as Darel Rutherford points out in *Being the Solution:*

The principles of miracles show us that the correct order of the creative process is not "Do, Have, Be" but, rather, "Be, Do, Have."

As we grow in the understanding of our true nature—of our spiritual heritage—and as we become increasingly aware of the spiritual support available to us, we become increasingly better able to "Be" the person who deserves miracles.

As we are able to "Be" this person, we automatically are energized to "Do" the things that move us toward our goal. We are divinely guided and directed, and that which we need is drawn to us.

And as we "Do" these things, not only do we "Have" that which we desire, even more importantly, we increasingly experience the quality of life and livingness that we most aspire to; we like ourselves better; we like others better; we are healthier; we have more successful relationships; our problems diminish; and we find great joy in our daily living.

What actually happens is that meditation calls forth the spiritual qualities inherent in each of us. These qualities are Life, Love, Light, Power, Peace, Beauty and Joy. These are the qualities of Spirit.[4] They are also centered in us, and it is the spiritual birthright of each of us to express them.

Not only are the effects of meditation long-lasting, they're cumulative as well. Answers come to us. This is why meditation leads to clarity of thought and intuitive insights. Solutions become obvious. We see possibilities we never thought of before. The "still, small voice" speaks softly, urging us forward. The more we listen to it, the more clearly it speaks. This is Spirit in action.

There are many different ways to meditate. Some people use a mantra, some chant, some meditate upon something and some attempt to keep their minds clear. I will share my own practice, as well as another that I know has been successfully used by many others.

First, however, keep in mind these important suggestions:

1. Try to meditate at the same time(s) every day.
2. Select a comfortable place.
3. Wear loose, comfortable clothing.
4. Ensure your back, spine and neck are in alignment.

5. Avoid interruptions. Meditation is a time for solitude.

Some people like to use candles and/or incense. Others use meditative music. These are not a part of my own practice, but if you find these things improve your meditative environment, by all means incorporate them into your routine.

After you are comfortably settled in your meditation space:

The first thing to do is to relax completely.

Feel a wave of relaxation wash over your entire body. Especially, relax your forehead, your eyes, your jaw— even your ears. Slowly and progressively relax your entire body, all the way from the top of your head down to your toes.

This relaxation takes us away from our focus on the outer world and opens us to new avenues through which our miracles may want to come. *Essentially, we are opening to the Infinite.*

Next, focus on your breathing.

Your breathing should be regular, with equal-length inhalations and exhalations. Make your breathing almost like a loop—in and out, in and out. This serves to shift our focus from the outer world to the inner world.

At this point, I will suggest two approaches. Try them both and use the one you like best. I like to say something like this:

"I am entering the sea of Beingness."[5]

I repeat this to myself a few times, softly at first, and then silently, until I feel myself shift to a higher level. (After some practice, this happens rather quickly.) Then, I focus the rest of the meditation on *one* of the qualities of Spirit. There are seven—Life, Love, Light, Power, Peace, Beauty and Joy—one for every day of the week. I spend the rest of my meditative time focusing on the "quality of the day," knowing that just as it is an essential quality of Spirit, so it is also an inherent quality in me. I focus on expressing it, visualizing it, being it, feeling it and receiving it.

When I slowly move out of my meditation, I like to go into affirmative prayer, which I discuss later in this chapter.

Another method that has been effective for many people is to do the relaxation and focus on the breathing, but instead of moving to concentrating on a Spiritual quality, this time:

Remain focused on your breathing.

As you inhale, be aware of the coolness inside the tip of your nose, and as you exhale be aware of the warmth and moisture. After a few minutes, focus on breathing in one nostril and breathing out the other. Remain focused on your breathing.[6]

With either of these meditative practices, if your attention wanders from either your breathing or the Spiritual quality on which you are concentrating, bring it gently back to your focus. If an uninvited thought makes its way into your consciousness, simply let it go right on through. If it seems persistent, tell it you'll give it your attention when you finish your meditation/affirmative prayer time. Then refocus your attention back to where you were. Do this gently and as often as necessary. As with so many other things we've discussed, this becomes progressively easier with practice.

> Meditate for whatever
> period of time is comfortable.

Many people meditate for anywhere from fifteen to thirty minutes twice a day. That might be a lot to start with, and you could find it hard to keep up with that schedule. So, start with five minutes at first or even three minutes. Build up slowly, but start, and be regular and consistent.

If twice a day doesn't work for you, do it once a day. There's no wrong way. Do whatever works best and modify it as needed. With all of these things, you will probably adapt slowly and gradually to a practice that is just right for you.

It's not necessary or important that you "feel" anything special during your meditation. Many people don't. There's nothing you're supposed to "get." What you're supposed to do is just "Be." It's not unusual, however, for regular meditators to experience lots of energy, or a feeling of overwhelming joy or recognition of unity at an almost transcendent level. Sometimes people feel a "click" of connection with the Universal.

Every person's meditation is personal and individual. There is nothing you can do that is wrong, nothing that you are missing.

> You're getting exactly what you're supposed to get, and it will change and progress as you continue with this practice.

You will also find that as you begin to develop your own meditation practice, you will "happen" to see articles and books that offer just the perfect idea for you to further develop your practice. This, too, is Spirit at work. Enjoy it.

AFFIRMATIVE PRAYER

Affirmative Prayer is covered in detail beginning on page 144 in Chapter 6. Hopefully, you are becoming, or have already become, familiar and comfortable with your own prayer style, either affirmative prayer or something else.

So just one reminder here: Please get in the habit of doing your prayer work out loud. It makes a big difference in the clarity of your thinking as you pray. It also increases your emotional involvement in the prayer.

You may remember that item 4 in the steps of affirmative prayer (pages 150-151) suggests a few moments of visualization. This is a very important part of your prayer.

VISUALIZATION

Visualization can be part of meditation. It can be part of affirmative prayer. It can be a separate practice of its own with its own private time, or it can even be practiced on and off throughout the day. It can be all of these in the same day.

Visualization, like meditation, is a practice in which many people at first are concerned that they either don't know how to do it or don't know how to do it right. There are many ways of visualizing, and there's nothing wrong with any of them. We're individuals, remember? We think *differently.* Some of us are visually oriented, and we can "see" images in our minds very clearly. Others of us don't "see" anything. Instead, we may "feel" them or simply "experience" them in some inner way.

So relax and enjoy the visualization process, however it is for you. It's very simple.

1. **Be very clear.** The more detail you can give your visualization, the better.

   For example, see (or imagine) your new business at its wonderful new location. Open the door and walk in. Go into your own office, beau-

tifully furnished; notice the color of the carpeting; admire the wall decorations. See all the new business orders in your "In" basket. Feel the excitement of this marvelous company that is benefiting so many people.

2. **Visualize your completed demonstration often.** Use different approaches. Close your eyes and put yourself in the finished picture.

If your miracle is for a beautiful new home, see yourself swimming in the pool behind your new home; see yourself entertaining on the spacious patio. If you are visualizing a recovery to good health, remember Virginia in Chapter 4 and visualize the doctor giving you good news; or, simply see yourself walking along just brimming with good health, enjoying the beauty of the surroundings. When you become fully accustomed to your return to good health, then see yourself on the tennis court. Feel your smooth backhand return that sends the ball just over the net, and feel the exhilaration resulting from a good volley. Or whatever it is for you.

3. **Make it real.** Do this by experiencing the positive emotion of the completed demonstration. In addition, enjoy every moment of your demonstration while it is unfolding. Give it lots of positive energy.

For example, for a reconciled relationship, you might see yourself having lunch with your father from whom you have been estranged. See the relaxed, warm look on his face; notice his tie, his suit, his haircut; and feel the warmth of reconciliation throughout your entire body. For a successful performance, imagine yourself taking the final bow to the audience following your wonderful piano concert. Hear the applause, then hear the cheers joining the applause. See the audience rise to its feet as you smile and bow. Simply imagine the marvelous feeling of having just given a peak performance.

Another nice thing about visualization is that you can visualize positively on a number of different things at different times throughout the day; or, if there's one major miracle that's on the way, visualize that throughout the day and regularly imagine this demonstration as already existing in your life.

Now you can take all the time you used to spend imagining all the bad things you thought "might happen" to you, and, instead, spend the same time creating wonderful new experiences in your life. How wonderful!

AFFIRMATIONS

Affirmations are short, positive statements of Truth. They are powerhouses of positive energy, and you can use them throughout the day. You can use them when you're brushing your teeth, dressing, driving, walking, waiting in line—just about anywhere and everywhere. They're especially helpful whenever you're facing a challenge. Most of the people you read about in this book used affirmations—a lot.

Affirmations have three things in common:

- They are short.
- They are positive.
- They are in the present tense.

They're short so they can be easily, frequently and powerfully repeated—either silently or out loud. They're positive, because you're establishing what you want, and not what you don't want. And they're in the present tense because you are establishing something new, and in the invisible realm (which is where the manifestation begins, right?) you are establishing it *right now.*

All too often, in affirmations as well as in affirmative prayer, people tend to use the future tense, e.g., "I *will* find the right and perfect new home" rather than "*I am finding* the right and perfect new home now." Remember, if you ask for something in the future tense, that's where it stays—in the future.

Essentially, affirmations do two things. First, they immediately shift our thinking from negative to positive. For example, the salesman may say to himself whenever he anticipates the big appointment, "My presentation is wonderful, and this is a perfect presentation." Or the person waiting for his performance evaluation says to him/herself, "There is excellent communication both ways during this evaluation. I am calm and confident knowing that only good comes out of it."

Two of my personal favorite affirmations are:

Right where I am, God is.

and

I am divinely guided, guarded, directed and protected.

The second thing affirmations do is to provide positive direction for the creative action of Spirit which is bringing to you the miracle you have specified.

Remember:

We direct, Spirit responds.

When faced with a health challenge, you might affirm something like, "I accept my perfect health right now." If the challenge is financial, you might say, "I give thanks for the prosperous abundance that is mine right now."

Don't be afraid to use affirmations. Think them, speak them, sing them, chant them, but use them, and use them often.

Your personal use of these suggestions constitutes your own spiritual practice. As you work with them, you will find that your practice unfolds smoothly and that it moves easily into a twenty-four-hour-a-day mantle of guidance and protection for you—wherever you are and wherever you go.

EPILOGUE

By now, dear reader, I'm sure you understand that the whole point of all the "clear thinking" is so that, to the greatest degree possible, you can relate to your Source, the Ultimate Observer, That Which Created You. As you release negative thoughts, feelings and emotions about yourself and others, you grow in consciousness and Spiritual unfoldment.

Your positive thoughts about yourself spring up around you as the good that you desire—as miracles in your world and in the world of others. And, best of all, because it all comes from One Infinite Source, there is absolutely no limit to this good.

It really is simple, isn't it?

Now it's up to *you*. You have a wonderful new way to look at yourself, your relationships, your world and your future. You are here to express life to whatever extent you desire. You are fully supported in all that you do. You are fully loved in all that you do—or don't do.

This is your life. Live it fully. Enjoy it.
You are not ordinary.
You are unique. You are one of a kind.

There is no one else like you, and there never will be. Sing your song, even if you are the only one who hears it.

It's a beautiful song, and it's yours alone. If you sing it for the whole world, that's good too, because that will be your choice and then others can enjoy it, too. You are supported in your choice by a loving Presence that provides—without question and all the time—all you could ever want or need.

Right where you are, there are many, many miracles. They are already yours!

APPENDIX

THE DOUBLE-SLIT EXPERIMENT

This experiment is the one most frequently used to explain and illustrate, among other things, the role of observation in the quantum world, and it is described by Margaret J. Wheatley in *Leadership and the New Science*, as follows:

> *"Most simply, this experiment involves electrons (or any other elementary particles) that must pass through one of two openings (slits) in a surface. After passing through one of these slits, each electron lands on a second surface, where its landing is recorded. A single electron passes through only one of the openings, but how it displays itself on the landing surface is affected by whether one or both slits are open at the time it passes through either one of them.*

> *"The electron, like all quantum entities, has two forms of being; it is both a wave and a particle. If both slits are open, the single electron acts as a wave, creating a pattern on the recording screen typical of the diffusion caused by a wave. If only one slit is open, the resulting pattern is that of discrete points, or the behavior of a particle.*

"On its way through one slit, the electron acts in a way that indicates it 'knows' whether or not the second hole is open. It knows what the scientist is observing for and adjusts its behavior accordingly. If the observer tries to 'fool' the subject by opening and shutting slits as the electron approaches the wall, the electron behaves in a manner appropriate for the state of the holes at the moment it passes through one."[*1]

Further, the electron even knows if the observer is watching. When the recording apparatus is off and the electron is not being observed and recorded, it exists only as a probability wave. According to prominent cosmologist John Gribbin, unless someone is watching, "nature herself does not know which hole the electron is going through."[2]

The following commentary regarding the double-slit experiment is taken from personal correspondence between the authors and Anthony S. Arrott, Ph.D., F.R.S.C., Professor Emeritus, Physics Department, Simon Fraser University, Vancouver, B.C.

"Yes, the double-slit experiment is very important for your readers. By way of some background information, it was first performed by Thomas Young in 1801. This showed the wave nature of light (photons). In 1839, Louis

---

*For those readers who are really interested in learning more about this experiment, it is presented in even greater detail in John Gribbin's, *In Search of Schroedinger's Cat*, on pages 166-174.

Daguerre invented photography which works by light activating single grains of silver halide. If anyone had bothered to think about it, the full mystery of quantum physics was now there for all to see... but none did. Light, which is a wave, acts like a particle when it hits and activates a grain of silver halide. If one takes a picture of Young's experiment, the picture is created one grain at a time. A particle of light is absorbed by the grain. Yet that particle acts like a wave on going through the double slit. This is the fundamental mystery. It remains a mystery.

"The fact that a photograph of the double-slit experiment is created one grain at a time is related to Einstein's photo-electric effect for which he got the Nobel Prize, eighty years after Daguerre's invention. The mystery of quantum physics is there in its full glory in the double-slit experiment. If you try to find out which slit the photon goes through, you lose the diffraction pattern. This is true for the photon and it is true for each of the fundamental particles, and it can be observed even using atoms and small molecules. The mystery of the double-slit experiment and the detection of the diffraction pattern using photography underlie all of quantum physics. Yet it took a generation of physicists starting with Einstein to realize what a mystery it is."

NOTES

Chapter 1

1. Page 6. William Hauck, *The Emerald Tablet: Alchemy for Personal Transformation* (New York: Penguin Arkana, 1999), p. 51.

2. Page 7. Hauck, *The Emerald Tablet,* p. 54.

Chapter 2

Prologue, Page 14. 1. The information contained in "The Miracle of our Universe and of Life Itself" was compiled from several sources. They are:

Robert Jastrow, *God and the* Astronomers (Second Edition) (New York/London: W. W. Norton & Company, 1992), pp. 10, 11, 29, 31, 92;

David Filkin, *Steven Hawking's Universe: The Cosmos Explained* (New York: HarperCollins, 1997), pp. 154-156;

Steven Hawking, *A Brief History of Time: From the Big Bang to Black Holes* (Toronto: Bantam Books, 1988), p. 121;

Alan Guth, *The Inflationary Universe: The Quest for a New Theory of Cosmic Origins* (New York: Perseus Books Group, 1998), p. 286; and also Alan Guth at http://www.edge.org/3rd_culture/guth02_index.html

1. Page 16. David Filkin, *Steven Hawking's Universe,* pp. 154, 155.

2. Page 16. Steven Hawking, *A Brief History of Time*, p. 124.

3. Page 18. Ralph Waldo Emerson, *Emerson's Essays, "History"* (New York: Harper & Row, 1926), p. 1.

4. Page 21. Bill Bryson, *A Short History of Nearly Everything* (New York, Broadway Books, 2003), p. 121.

5. Page 23. Steven Hawking, *A Brief History of Time*, p. 29.

6. Page 25. This story is recounted by Robert Jastrow in *God and the Astronomers,* pp. 18 – 21, and also by David Filkin in *Steven Hawking's Universe,* pp. 83-86.

7. Page 28. Robert Jastrow, *God and the Astronomers,* p. 26.

Chapter 3

1. Page 32. Richard P. Feynman, *Six Easy Pieces: Essentials to Physics Explained by its Most Brilliant Teacher* (New York: Helix Books, 1995), p. 4.

2. Page 32. Bill Bryson, *A Short History of Nearly Everything*, p. 134.

3. Page 33. Deepak Chopra, *How to Know God: The Soul's Journey into the Mystery of Mysteries* (New York: Harmony Books, 2000), p. 11.

4. Page 35. James Jeans, *The Mysterious Universe* (New York: Macmillan Co., 1948), p. 166, 186.

5. Page 37. Fritjof Capra, *The Tao of Physics: An Exploration of the Parallels Between Modern Physics and Eastern Mysticism* (Boulder: Shambhala, 1975), p. 141.

6. Page 39. John Peat and David F. Briggs, *Turbulent Mirror: An Illustrated Guide to Chaos Theory and the Science of Wholeness* (New York: Harper & Row, 1990), p. 29.

7. Page 39. Steven Hawking, *A Brief History of Time*, p. 56.

8. Page 39. Margaret J. Wheatley, *Leadership and the New Science: Discovering Order in a Chaotic World*, 2nd Ed. (San Francisco: Berrett-Kohler, 1999), p. 33.

9. Page 39. John Gribbin, *In Search of Schroedinger's Cat: Quantum Physics and Reality* (New York: Bantam Books, 1984), p, 5.

10. Page 40. Gary Zukav, *The Dancing Wu Li Masters: An Overview of the New Physics* (New York: Bantam Books, 1984), p. 51.

11. Page 40. Margaret J. Wheatley, *Leadership and the New Science*, p. 64.

12. Page 45. Steven Hawking, *A Brief History of Time*, p. 55.

13. Page 48. Larry Dossey, M.D., *Space, Time and Medicine* (Boston, Shambhala, 1982), p. 98.

14. Page 51. Robert G. Jahn and Brenda J. Dunne, *Margins of Reality: The Role of Consciousness in the Physical World* (SanDiego, New York, London: Harcourt Brace Jovanovich, 1987), p. 211.

15. Page 52. Larry Dossey, M.D., *Space, Time and Medicine*, p. 102.

16. Page 52. Edgar Mitchell, *The Way of the Explorer* (New York: G. P. Putnam's Sons, 1996), p. 111.

17. Page 52. J. K. Wheeler, K. S. Thorne and C. Misner, *Gravitation* (San Francisco: Freeman, 1973), p. 173.

18. Page 53. Larry Dossey, M.D., *Space, Time and Medicine*, p. 132.

19. Page 53. Larry Dossey, M.D., *Space, Time and Medicine*, p. 132.

Chapter 4

1. Page 72. Chad Helmstetter, *What to Say When You Talk to Yourself* (New York: Bantam Books, 1982), pp. 63-71.

2. Page 74. Maxwell Maltz, M.D., *PsychoCybernetics* (New York: Pocket Books, 1960), pp. 7, 8.

Chapter 5

1. Page 93. David D. Burns, M.D, *Freeling Good: The New Mood Therapy* (New York: Quill, 2000), p. xx.

2. Page 93. David D. Burns, M.D., *Feeling Good,* p. xxi.

3. Page 115. Tian of Siam, *Quam* (Kearney, Neb.: Morris Publishing, 2001), p. 37.

4. Page 116. Tian of Siam, *Quam,* p. 38.

Chapter 6

1. Pages 127, 128. The story of Buckminster Fuller was taken from several sources, including Hatch, Alden, *Buckminster Fuller: At Home in the Universe* (New York: Crown Publishers, Inc., 1974); also the one-man show, "R. Buckminster Fuller: The History (and Mystery) of the Universe," written and directed by D. W. Jacobs, performed by Ron Campbell; also, http://www.bfi.org/introduction_to_bmf.htm.

2. Page 146. "New Scientific Proof: Prayer Really Can Work Miracles!" *Woman's World*, Englewood Cliffs, N.J., August 13, 2002, p. 14.

3. Page 146. *Woman's World*, August 13, 2002, p. 15.

4. Page 146. *Woman's World,* August 13, 2002, p. 15.

5. Page 147. *Woman's World*, August 13, 2002, p. 14, and Roger A. Lobo, M.D., "Does Prayer Influence the Success of In Vitro Fertilization/Embryo Transfer? (IVF-ET)," *Journal of Reproductive Medicine* (Vol. 46, 2001), p. 781.

Chapter 7

1. Page 159. Masaru Emoto, *The Hidden Messages in Water* (Hillsboro, OR: Beyond Words Publishing, Inc. 2004), p. xxv.
2. Page 161. Larry Dossey, *Space, Time and Medicine*, p. 74.
3. Page 161. Larry Dossey, *Space, Time and Medicine*, p. 74.
4. Page 162. Doc Lew Childre and Martin Howard, *The Heartmath® Solution: The Institute of Heartmath's Revolutionary Program for Engaging the Power of the Heart's Intelligence* (Harper-SanFrancisco, a Division of HarperCollinsPublishers, 2000), p. 59.
5. Page 162. Doc Lew Childre and Martin Howard, *The Heartmath® Solution*, p. 33.
6. Page 171. Rollin McCraty, Ph.D., Mike Atkinson, and Dana Tomasino, B.A. et al "Modulation of DNA Conformation by Heart Focused Intention," Heartmath Research Center, Institute of Heartmath, Publication No. 03-008 (Boulder Creek, CA), 2003.
7. Page 175. The one-man show, "R. Buckminster Fuller," written and directed by D. W. Jacobs.
8. Pages 178–180. Charles R. Walgreen's story was taken from the following websites: http://www.lib.niu.edu/ipo/ihy000443.html; http://www.walgreens.com/about/history/default.jhtml; and http://www.walgreens.com/about/history/hist6.jhtml.

Chapter 8

1. Page 187. Raymond Charles Barker, *Treat Yourself to Life* (New York: Dodd, Mead & Company, 1988), p. 23.

Chapter 9

1. Page 219. Information on Hans Selye taken from the following website: http://collections.ic.gc.ca/heirloom_series/volume4/222-223.html.
2. Page 228. Gerald Jampolsky, M.D., *Goodbye to Guilt: Releasing Fear Through Forgiveness* (New York, Bantam Books, 1985), p. 134.
3. Page 229. Gerald Jampolsky, M.D., *Goodbye to Guilt*, p. 135.
4. Page 241. Dr. Fred Luskin, *Forgive for Good: A Proven Prescription for Health and Happiness* (SanFrancisco: HarperSanFrancisco, 2002), xvii.

Chapter 11

1. Page 275. The story of Mohini the white tiger was taken from *Abundant Living.* This newsletter was published by Delia Sellers Ministries, Vol. 14, No. 3 (Prescott, AZ, 2004).

2. Page 279. Ina Albert and Zoe Keithley, *Write Yourself Well ... Journal Yourself to Health* (WhiteFish, Mo., Mountain Greenery Press, 2004), *pp. 7- 9.*

3. Page 280. *Woman's World,* August 13, 2002, p. 15.

4. Page 282. Thomas Troward, *The Creative Process in the Individual* (New York: Dodd, Mead & Company, 1915), pp. 67, 68.

5. Page 284. Thank you, Dr. Don Burt.

6. Page 284. Blair Lewis, PA-C *Meditation: The Inward Journey* eBook (www.AliveandHealthy.com), Alive and Healthy Foundation 2003), p. 21.

Appendix A

1. Pages 295, 296. Margaret J. Wheatley, *Leadership and the New Science,* pp. 63, 64. Reprinted with permission of the publisher. All rights reserved. (www.bkconnection.com)

BIBLIOGRAPHY

Abundant Living. Delia Sellers Ministries. Vol. 14, No. 3, March. Prescott, Arizona: 2004.

Albert, Ina and Keithley, Zoe. *Write Your Self Well... Journal Your Self to Health.* White Fish, Mo.: Mountain Greenery Press, 2004.

Bailes, Dr. Frederick. *Basic Principles of the Science of Mind,* 3rd ed. Marina del Rey, Ca.: DeVorss & Company, 1980.

Barker, Raymond Charles. *Treat Yourself to Life.* New York: Dodd, Mead & Company, 1988.

Bodanis, David. $E = mc^2$, *A Biography of the World's Most Famous Equation.* New York: Berkeley Books, 2000.

Boorse, Henry A., Lloyd, Motz, and Jefferson, Hane Weaver. *The Atomic Scientists: A Biographical History.* New York: John Wiley & Sons, Inc.,1989.

Borysenko, Joan. *Guilt Is the Teacher, Love Is the Lesson.* New York: Warner Brothers, 1991.

Braden, Gregg. *The Isaiah Effect: Decoding the Lost Science of Prayer and Prophecy.* New York: Three Rivers Press, 2000.

Briggs, John and Peat, F. David. *Turbulent Mirror: An Illustrated Guide to Chaos Theory and the Science of Wholeness.* New York: Harper & Row, 1990.

Bryson, Bill. *A Short History of Nearly Everything.* New York: Broadway Books, 2003.

Burns, David D., M.D. *Feeling Good: The New Mood Therapy.* New York: Quill, 2000.

Butterworth, Eric. *Discover the Power Within You: A Guide to the Unexplored Power Within.* San Francisco: HarperSanFrancisco, 1968, 1989.

Capacchione, Lucia, Ph.D. *Visioning: Ten Steps to Designing the Life of Your Dreams.* New York: Jeremy P. Tarcher, 2000.

——————. *Recovery of Your Inner Child: The Highly Acclaimed Method for Liberating Your Inner Self.* New York: Fireside, 1991.

Capra, Fritjof. *The Web of Life.* New York: Anchor Books/Doubleday, 1996.

303

——————. *The Tao of Physics: An Exploration of the Parallels Between Modern Physics and Eastern Mysticism.* Boulder: Shambhala, 1975.

Childre, Doc Lew, and Martin, Howard. *The Heartmath® Solution: The Institute of HeartMath's Revolutionary Program for Engaging the Power of the Heart's Intelligence.* HarperSanFrancisco: A Division of HarperCollinsPublishers, 2000.

Chopra, Deepak. *How to Know God: The Soul's Journey Into The Mystery of Mysteries.* New York: Harmony Books, 2000.

——————. *The Seven Spiritual Laws of Success.* San Rafael, Ca.: Amber-Allen Publishing and New World Library, 1994.

——————. *Ageless Body, Timeless Mind: The Quantum Alternative to Growing Old.* New York: Harmony Books, 1993.

Conwell, Russell H. *Acres of Diamonds.* New York: Jove Books, 2000.

Dossey, Larry, M.D. *Be Careful What You Pray For...: You Just Might Get It.* San Francisco: HarperSanFrancisco, 1978.

——————. *Healing Words: The Power of Prayer and the Practice of Medicine.* San Francisco: HarperSanFrancisco, 1993.

——————. *Space, Time & Medicine.* Boston: Shambhala, 1982.

Dresser, Horatio W. *The Quimby Manuscripts.* New York: The Julian Press, 1961.

Eddington, A.S. *The Nature of the Physical World.* New York: The Macmillan Company, 1930.

Emoto, Masaru. *The Hidden Messages in Water.* Hillsboro, or: Beyond Words Publishing, Inc., 2004.

Emerson, Ralph Waldo. *Emerson's Essays.* "History." New York: Harper & Row Publishers, 1926.

Feynman, Richard, P. *Six Easy Pieces: Essentials of Physics Explained by Its Most Brilliant Teacher.* New York: Helix Books, 1995.

Fezler, William, Ph.D. *Creative Imagery: How to Visualize in All Five Senses.* New York: Fireside, 1989.

Filkin, David. *Steven Hawking's Universe: The Cosmos Explained.* New York: HarperCollins, 1997.

Freke, Timothy, and Gandy, Peter. *The Hermetica: The Lost Wisdom of the Pharaohs.* New York: Penguin Putnam, Inc., 1997.

Gawain, Shakti. *Creative Visualization,* rev. ed. Novato, Ca.: Nataraj Publishing, 1995.

Goswami, Amit. *The Self-Aware Universe: How Consciousness Creates the Material World,* New York: Jeremy P. Tarcher, 1993.

Greene, Brian. *The Elegant Universe: Superstrings, Hidden Dimensions, and the Quest for the Ultimate Theory.* New York: Vintage Books, 2000.

Gribbin, John. *Almost Everyone's Guide to Science: The Universe, Life and Everything.* New Haven, Ct., and London: Yale University Press, 1998.

—————————. *In Search of Schroedinger's Cat: Quantum Physics and Reality.* New York: Bantam Books, 1984.

Guth, Alan. *The Inflametory Universe: The Quest for a New Theory of Cosmic Origins.* New York: Perseus Book Group, 1998.

Hansen, Mark Victor and Batten, Joe D. *The Master Motivator.* Deerfield Beach, Fla.: Health Communications, Inc., 1995.

Hatch, Alden. *Buckminster Fuller: At Home in the Universe.* New York: Crown Publishers, Inc., 1974.

Hauck, William. *The Emerald Tablet: Alchemy for Personal Transformation.* New York: Penguin Arkana, 1999.

Hawking, Stephen W. *A Brief History of Time: From the Big Bang to Black Holes.* Toronto: Bantam Books, 1988.

—————————. *The Universe in a Nutshell.* New York: Bantam Books, 2001.

Helmstetter, Shad, Ph.D. *What to Say When You Talk to Yourself.* New York: Bantam Books, 1982.

Holmes, Ernest. *The Anatomy of Healing Prayer.* Marina del Rey, Ca.: DeVorss Publications, 1991.

—————————. *How to Use The Science of Mind.* New York: Dodd, Mead & Company, 1980.

—————————. *Ideas of Power.* Marina del Rey, Ca.: DeVorss Publications, 1992.

—————————. *The Science of Mind,* 50th ed. New York: G. Putnam's Sons, 1988.

Jacobs, D. W., writer and director of the one-man show, "R. Buckminster Fuller: The History (and Mystery) of the Universe." performed by Ron Campbell.

Jahn, Robert G. and Dunne, Brenda J. *Margins of Reality: The Role of Consciousness in the Physical World.* San Diego/New York/London: Harcourt Brace Jovanovich, 1987.

Jammer, Max. *Einstein and Religion: Physics and Theology*. Princeton: Princeton University Press, 1999.

Jampolsky, Gerald, M.D. *Good-Bye to Guilt: Releasing Fear through Forgiveness*. New York: Bantam Books, 1985.

Jastrow, Robert. *God and the Astronomers (Second Edition)*. New York/London: W. W. Norton & Company, Inc., 1992.

Jeans, James. *The Mysterious Universe*. New York: The Macmillan Co., 1948.

Jeffers, Susan, Ph.D. *Feel The Fear and Do It Anyway*. New York: Fawcett Columbine, 1987.

—————————. *Embracing Uncertainty: Breakthrough Methods for Achieving Peace of Mind When Facing the Unknown*. New York: St. Martin's Press, 2003.

Kenny, Anthony, Editor. *The Oxford History of Western Philosophy*. New York: Oxford University Press, 1994.

Klein, Charles. *How to Forgive When You Can't Forget: Healing Our Personal Relationships*. New York: Berkley Books, 1995.

Lederman, Leon and Teresi, Dick. *The God Particle: If the Universe is the Answer, What is the Question?* New York: Dell Publishing, 1993.

Levoy, Gregg. *Callings: Finding and Following an Authentic Life*. New York: Three Rivers Press, 1997.

Luskin, Fred, Dr. *Forgive for Good: A Proven Prescription for Health and Happiness*. SanFrancisco: HarperSanFrancisco, 2002.

Maltz, Maxwell, M.D. *Psycho-Cybernetics*. New York et. al.: Pocket Books, 1960.

McCraty, Rollin. Ph.D., Atkinson, Mike and Tomosino, Dana, B.A., et.al. "Modulation of DNA Conformation by Heart Focused Intention." Heartmath Research Center, Institute of Heartmath, Publication No. 03-008: Boulder Creek, 2003.

McTaggart, Lynne. *The Field: The Quest for the Secret Force of the Universe*. New York: Quill, 2002.

Mitchell, Dr. Edgar. *The Way of the Explorer*. New York: G. P. Putnam's Sons, 1996.

Murphy, Joseph. *The Power of Your Subconscious Mind*. Paramus, N.J.: Prentice Hall, 1963.

Oldfield, Ruth. *Albert Einstein: Man of Science*. Chicago: Children's Press, 1964.

Oyle, Irving, Dr. *Time, Space & the Mind.* Millbrae, Ca.: Celestial Arts, 1976.

Progoff, Ira. *At An Intensive Journal® Workshop: Writing to Access the Power of the Unconscious and Evoke Creative Ability.* New York: G. P. Putnam's Sons, 1992.

Ricard, Matthieu and Thuan, Trinh Xuan. *The Quantum and the Lotus.* New York: Crown Publishers, 2001.

Rutherford, Darel. *Being the Solution: A Spiritual Path to Personal Power and Financial Independence,* Albuquerque, N.M.: DAR Publishing, 2002.

Siegel, Bernie S., M. D. *Peace, Love & Healing.* New York: HarperPerennial, 1989.

Simonton, O. Carl, M.D. et al. *Getting Well Again.* New York: J. P. Tarcher, 1978.

Smedes, Lewis B. *Forgive & Forget: Healing the Hurts We Don't Deserve.* New York: Pocket Books, 1984.

Snow, C. P. *The Physicists.* London: House of Stratus, 2001.

Starcke, Walter. *It's All God.* Boerne, Texas: Guadalupe Press, 1998.

——————————. *The Double Thread.* Boerne, Texas: Guadalupe Press, 1967.

Thuan, Trinh Xuan. *The Birth of the Universe.* New York: Harry N. Abrams, 1993.

Tian of Siam. *Quam.* Kearney, Neb: Morris Publishing, 2001

Tipping, Colin. *Radical Forgiveness: Making Room for the Miracle,* 2nd ed. Marietta, Ga.: Global 13 Publications, Inc., 2002.

Troward, Thomas. *The Creative Process in the Individual.* New York: Dodd, Mead & Company, 1915.

——————————. *The Edinburgh Lectures.* New York: Dodd, Mead & Company, 1909.

——————————. *The Hidden Power.* New York: Dodd, Mead & Company, 1921.

——————————. *The Law and The Word.* New York: Dodd, Mead & Company, 1917.

Walker, Evan Harris. *The Physics of Consciousness, the Quantum Mind and the Meaning of Life.* Cambridge, Mass.: Perseus Publishing, 2000.

Walsh, Neale Donald. *Conversations With God: An Uncommon Dialogue,*

Book 2. Charlottesville, Va.: Hampton Roads Publishing Company, Inc., 1997.

Walsh, Roger, M.D., Ph.D. *Essential Spirituality: The 7 Central Practices to Awaken Heart and Mind.* New York: John Wiley & Sons, Inc., 1999.

Walters, Donald J., *Intuition for Starters: How to Know and Trust Your Inner Guidance.* Nevada City, Ca.: Crystal Clarity Publishers, 2003.

Wheatley, Margaret J. *Leadership and the New Science,* 2nd ed. San Francisco: Berrett-Koehler, 1999.

Wheeler, J. A., Thorne, K. S. and Misner, C., *Gravitation.* San Francisco: Freeman, 1973.

Whitehead, Carleton. *Creative Meditation.* New York: Dodd, Mead & Company, 1975.

Whitfield, Charles L., M.D. *Healing the Child Within: Discovery and Recovery for Adult Children of Dysfunctional Families.* Deerfield Beach, Fla.: Health Communications, Inc., 1987.

Zukav, Gary. *The Dancing Wu Li Masters: An Overview of the New Physics.* New York: Bantam Books, 1984.

ACKNOWLEDGMENTS

We gratefully and lovingly acknowledge Dr. Ernest Holmes, author of *The Science of Mind* and many other outstanding books, for his lifelong quest for Truth. We believe that the results of this search are reflected on every page of this book.

Each one of the many clients we have worked with has contributed greatly to this book. We have changed the names of those whose stories we used, but all of you—and you know who you are—have been an important part of our experience. We have learned from you that these principles do work and that lives really change for the better when we change consciousness and begin to realize the Truth of our being.

We deeply appreciate the many hours of time and attention spent on this book by both Zoe Keithley and Michael Seman—as well as their wonderful suggestions. Their ideas were important and meaningful, and made us think more deeply.

Many people have been supportive of our work as it was unfolding and, in particular, we thank Dr. Marva White for her consistent encouragement.

Special thanks to Anthony S. Arrott, Ph.D., F.R.S.C., for reviewing our manuscript for technical accuracy and providing valuable guidance and insight regarding the current state of scientific knowledge. (Tony, too bad we couldn't include your wonderful humor.)

We have indeed been fortunate to have a literary agent as dedicated as Muriel Nellis. She never lost faith in us—even though it took us *so much* longer than we ever expected. Her constant support and encouragement have been indispensable. And Elizabeth Zack, our wonderful editor, added immeasurably to the clarity of the ideas we present here.

How fortunate we have been to have Susan Jeffers and Mark Shelmerdine see the possibilities of our book and decide they wanted to publish it. They have made everything go so smoothly and so joyously for us. We thank them and gratefully acknowledge them both.

Acknowledgments

We want to particularly acknowledge the wonderful research support of Kristine Gennero. She was always ready; always helping; always encouraging.

And, Bill Arrott, thank you again and again—for the hours of reading and re-reading as the manuscript unfolded, for the many helpful suggestions, and most of all for the enthusiastic support you gave both of us.

We are deeply honored to be able to present these ideas and teachings so that others may benefit from them.

ABOUT THE AUTHORS

Michael C. Rann and Elizabeth Rann Arrott are a former husband and wife team responsible for many outstanding successes in the Chicago marketing and advertising industry. They now bring the same energy and synergy to the literary world with *Shortcut to a Miracle*, their first book together.

Some thirty years ago, both Michael and (soon thereafter) Elizabeth began to study with some of the finest teachers of Science of Mind. Both are now teachers, practitioners and ministers of Religious Science International.

Michael is Pastor of the First Church of Religious Science in Chicago, and Elizabeth is Pastor of Religious Science of the North Shore in Evanston, Illinois. Michael has written two self-published booklets on the power of mind and spirit; *Something Good is About to Happen* and *The Power of Commitment*. Both Michael and Elizabeth dedicate their time to speaking, teaching, counseling and showing others what can be accomplished by using the mind in a positive way.

Elizabeth also serves as District President of the International New Thought Alliance for the states of Illinois and Wisconsin.

Michael is a graduate of DePaul University, School of Music, where he did both undergraduate and graduate work in preparation for a career in opera.

Elizabeth is a graduate of Michigan State University where she majored in both Literature and Psychology.

Both are charismatic and dynamic speakers whose philosophy of life is one of success—for themselves, their clients, and all those around them.

Although their marriage has ended, their working relationship continues to flourish—something many would consider a miracle in and of itself!

Michael and Elizabeth both live in Chicago, Illinois.

SHARE YOUR MIRACLE

We (the authors) expect that you will experience many miracles as a result of this book. We are considering a follow-up book that will incorporate some of the ways various people found this book helpful in making their life miraculous and how their individual miracles came about.

If you would like to share your miracle, we would love to hear about it.

Both of us are available—separately or together—for workshops and seminars.

Please contact us at:

Shortcut to a Miracle
P.O. Box 8285
Chicago, IL 60680